Phyllis Schlafly Speaks, Volume 1

# Her Favorite Speeches

Phyllis Schlafly

Edited by Ed Martin

ISBN 978-0-9984000-0-6

**Skellig**
**AMERICA**

# TABLE OF CONTENTS

## Editor's Note by Ed Martin

On September 5, 2016, Phyllis Schlafly died at the age of 92. A few years before her death, Phyllis Schlafly reviewed a catalogue of the thousands of speeches she had delivered. The catalogue, maintained at the Phyllis Schlafly Center in Clayton, Missouri, includes speeches given as far back as the 1950s that cover issues and topics from pro-life to missile defense to education and of course to politics and campaigns.

After this review, Phyllis selected a dozen of her favorites and asked that they be transcribed from the original audio or video. A few of the speeches that had not been recorded were edited from written speech notes. All of these speeches are in this book.

Phyllis Schlafly's output as a speaker and writer is so vast that it will take us decades to re-print what took her more than seven decades in public life to create. This is the first volume in what will be many volumes; her wisdom, wit and insight on nearly every subject of historical significance makes it a wonderful challenge for an editor.

The introduction of this book is a tribute that Laura Ingraham wrote just after Phyllis died. Laura was a friend of Phyllis – she admired Laura's wit, her class, her talent. Phyllis often mentioned, in speaking of Laura, her gratitude for the time that Laura stepped in to help at one of Phyllis' big events. Back in 2008, then-Alaska Governor Sarah Palin was to speak at Phyllis' quadrennial pro-life party at the Republican National Convention in St Paul, Minnesota. For reasons that later became clear (when Sarah was named to the presidential ticket), she cancelled her appearance at the last minute. Phyllis needed a substitute who could draw a crowd and give them a good speech. Laura stepped up and was a hit! Phyllis remembered her kindness fondly.

In addition, the last two chapters of this book are warm remembrances of Phyllis by two of her sons, John and Andy.

*Ed Martin*

## Dedication by Laura Ingraham

W hen I heard conservative icon Phyllis Schlafly had passed away yesterday at age 92, I stopped what I was doing with the kids, went into the bathroom and sobbed. What a friend! What a lady! What a fighter! What an inspiration! She was a standing rebuke to the lazy notion that conservative women are weaker than feminists. She was a true giant – one of the great figures of American history. Consider these facts.

On Oct. 12, 1971, the House passed the Equal Rights Amendment by a vote of 354-24. On March 22, 1972, it passed the Senate by a vote of 84-8. The Equal Rights Amendment would have opened the door to eliminating gender-specific bathrooms, put women on track for the draft, and revoked tax protections for dependent women not in the workforce. And it was supported by both parties' platforms. In 1972, the Democratic platform called for "a priority effort to ratify the Equal Rights Amendment."

The GOP platform also called for "ratification of the Equal Rights Amendment." By the end of 1973, 30 states had ratified the amendment – the ERA and its band of supporters only needed eight more. They never got them. Phyllis Schlafly, acting against overwhelming majorities in both Houses of Congress, the will of the president of the United States, and the desires of both parties, took on the ERA and its elite supporters – and beat them.

In 1978, with time running out (the ERA was supposed to be approved by 1979), Congress granted an extension until 1982. No new states approved the ERA during this time frame.

In my opinion, this is one of the greatest political victories ever won in American history. The odds against her, the importance of the issue, and the scale of her victory are almost impossible to overstate. And of course that's not all. She was an early supporter of Ronald Reagan, and we all know what he did. And to the end of her life, she kept fighting for her country.

She attended the 2016 Republican National Convention in Cleveland in a wheelchair, frail but as determined and feisty as ever. Warning anyone who would listen about the loss of our sovereignty and the Supreme Court, she supported Donald Trump when so many latter-day conservatives were turning up their noses at him. It should be noted that she did more for conservatism in one day than most of them will ever do in a lifetime.

She didn't mind being unfashionable. She didn't mind taking on Republicans. She didn't mind getting hammered in the press. She never gave up, never grew bitter, never let down her guard, and never quit doing her best. She was a standing rebuke to the lazy notion that conservative women are weaker than feminists.

The conservative icon died the day before her last book, "The Conservative Case for Trump," was released. The book will be the capstone on an incredible life spent fighting for conservatism – launched when Schlafly self-published her first book, "A Choice Not An Echo," that sold an incredible 3 million copies in 1964.

People should write books about her, and write poems about her, and make movies about her. She was an American hero – or, as she would probably prefer – heroine.

*This tribute column ran on Laura Ingraham's LifeZette.com, the digital news and commentary site started by Laura in 2015. It can be accessed at lifezette.com/polizette/my-hero-rip/.*

*Laura Ingraham joined FOX News Channel in 2007 and currently serves as a contributor, providing political analysis and commentary to FNC's daytime and primetime programming. She is the Editor-in-Chief of LifeZette.com. In addition to her role as a contributor, Ingraham is a frequent substitute host on FNC's "The O'Reilly Factor." As the host of the radio program "The Laura Ingraham Show," she is also the most listened-to woman in political talk radio in the United States, heard by hundreds of radio stations nationwide. Ingraham previously served as a litigator and Supreme Court law clerk.*

## May 7, 1990
## Washington, DC
## How Therapy Replaced Academics

I appreciate those kind words and I compliment your courage in inviting me here today. I hope they don't hold that against you and your career in this distinguished law firm. Seriously, I feel very honored to have the opportunity to talk to this particular group on what I think is the biggest issue out across the highways and byways of America. And that is what is going on in the public schools.

Now you've seen lots of reports in the papers about the dropouts and about the illiteracy. You may know that Al Shanker, the president of the second largest teachers union, said recently in a speech that, of those who do graduate from public high schools, only six percent can read a newspaper editorial, write a two-page essay, or do a two-step math problem. But that's not what I'm going to talk to you about today—how that happened or what to do about it. What I would like to devote these few minutes to is what is going on in the schools. Since they can't read, what are they doing all those hours in the public schools?

Starting back in the 1970s, there was a shift in the public schools away from the basics, away from subject content, toward a policy of probing the students' feelings and attitudes and opinions and emotions. The public school classroom became a place, not for learning, but for treating social problems. This was not done by a counselor on a one-on-one basis of troubled children. We're talking about what went on in the classroom. It became a kind of a "group therapy" of this captive group of minors. Nobody, of course, had consented to this type of therapy—not the students or the parents or the taxpayers.

What happened in the schools was best summarized by Sam Hayakawa, who was a university president before he became a U.S. Senator from the state of California. He said that it is an educational heresy—a heresy that rejects education as the acquisition of knowledge and skills, and instead regards the fundamental task of education as therapy. Hayakawa was the leader in the passage of a little-known federal law called the Protection of Pupil Rights Amendment, which passed nearly unanimously in 1978. It said that no student shall be required without parental consent to be subjected to psychological testing or treatment, to reveal information about political affiliations, problems embarrassing to the student or his family, sex behavior and attitudes, self-incriminating behavior, or critical appraisals of other family members. Now you recognize that no state official could ask you and compel your answer to those questions, but the fact that it was being done to public school children shows that this was a problem back in 1978 when the law was passed.

Because of the opposition of the education establishment of this law, it took six years for the regulations to be promulgated, which were done in 1984. We are now 12 years after the passage of this law, and it has never been enforced. At the same time, the problem that this law addressed has become pervasive. Some professionals even talk openly about what they call the "therapeutic classroom." I believe that what has happened in the classes not only violates this law, but it has risen to the level of a constitutional violation: violations where they invade the privacy rights of the pupil and his family through compelled disclosure of feelings, attitudes, opinions, and behaviors; secondly, a denial of their Fifth Amendment rights against self-incrimination; third, First Amendment violations through the use of quasi-religious exercises in class; and fourth, compelled psychological group treatment by teachers who are not trained in psychotherapy. I have, in my Eagle Forum Parents' Advisory Center, complaints from parents coming in daily from all fifty states. Let me give you some examples. First are the nosy questionnaires—this is one of the most prevalent tactics in the public schools. I give you as an example one that was used on Minnesota public school children in 1986. It was a one-hour, 189 question survey. First, there were the questions that invaded the privacy of the person. Are you a religious person? Are your parents divorced? Were they never married? Do you live in a house with a man to whom your mother is not related?

Then there were the questions to alienate the child from his parent. Would you like to see a doctor or nurse or counselor without your parents knowing about it? Then the child was asked: what are you worried about? Are you worried about dying soon? Being killed by a nuclear bomb? One parent dying, or your parents divorcing? Many questions were very depressing. Have you felt so sad, discouraged, hopeless, had so many problems that you wonder if anything is worthwhile? Are you worried about losing your mind or losing your memory? Have you had a nervous breakdown? Have you tried to kill yourself? There were many detailed questions on suicide. Then there were incriminating questions about the use of drugs. How often do you use cigarettes, beer, wine, hard liquor, marijuana, crack, cocaine, and a list of about twenty different drugs? There were questions on explicit sex. Have you had sexual intercourse? How old were you the first time you had it? Do you use birth control, and what kind? There was a detailed question to test the threshold of sensitivity to homosexual attraction.

Minnesota came back last year with a variation on this test, and gave it to all children in grades 6, 9, and 12. Again there were the privacy-invading questions: how often do you attend religious services? How important is religion in your life? There were threshold questions to test the threshold of sensitivity to religious commitment. There were questions that caused the child to inform on his parents: has alcohol by any family member caused health, job, or legal problems? Who caused it? Likewise, questions in regard to the use of drugs:

how old were you when you started using pot or other drugs? How often do you get drunk?

These questionnaires are obvious violations of the Protection of Pupil Rights Amendment, and the U.S. Department of Education has refused to act, although the complaints have been sitting there for over a year. These are not isolated cases; these questionnaires are everywhere.

I'll give you another example from Chapel Hill, North Carolina. A 200-question survey. First, they had the "True or False" downers: I want to kill myself; nothing is fun; I hate myself; I look ugly; I don't have any friends; I'm sure terrible things will happen to me. The child is to check "true" or "false." Then, there were the questions forcing the child to inform on his friends: name your best girlfriend and your best boyfriend, and then answer 47 questions about your relationship with these best friends. Name the kids you like the best and the ones you like the least, and those who do weird things.

Then, there were the questions that required the children to inform on their parents—22 questions on how parents react to good grades or bad grades on the report card; did any member of your family attempt suicide, divorce, remarry, or get arrested? What would you like to change about your house? Do your parents like their jobs? Then there were the questions that are incriminating to the student: how easy or hard is it for you to get cigarettes, pot, liquor or drugs?

In Texas, there was a self-description questionnaire in which the child was given 76 personal true or false statements. The child was to check "true" or "false": my parents are usually disappointed with what I do; most kids have more friends than I do; I am dumb in all school subjects.

In Alaska, we discovered an "AIDS Attitude" questionnaire. Again, it is testing the threshold of sensitivity to this subject. A child was given 54 statements and told to state whether he strongly agrees, agrees, disagrees, or strongly disagrees, such as: I would prefer not to be around homosexuals for fear of catching AIDS; I think people with AIDS get what they deserve.

In Maryland, parents discovered a questionnaire in which the child was asked: why don't you like to go to church? Why are you an outcast? What do your parents think of you?

Now these are all techniques of self-disclosure that compel the child to answer questions which are invasive of his personal and family privacy. And the questionnaires are not the only type. There are other methods, such as the nasty little game called "magic circle," in which the children are required to sit around in a circle and then they are induced to disclose their personal attitudes and opinions and to tell about private family matters. The noted business writer Peter Drucker has written eloquently an article to the *Wall Street Journal* about how harmful these public confessions are when employers force them on their employees. Drucker called them an invasion of privacy and morally indefensible. If they're bad for adults, what do you think about having them forced on children?

But this type of self-disclosure is not the only constitutional invasion of children in the public schools. Now let's talk about the psychological courses. And again, we're not talking about a counselor dealing on a one-on-one basis with a troubled child. We are talking about classroom courses that deal with the captive audience as a group, a type of group therapy. These courses are clearly psychological, and some of them are quasi-religious. They definitely use a lot of the practices and techniques that are common to the New Age ideology. If any of you have looked at the bookstores with the New Age racks, you will find very quickly that it is a religious movement and they have very clear techniques of practice in compliance with the New Age ideology.

Now let's talk about what's going on in the public school classroom involuntarily imposed upon little children. In kindergarten, first, and second grade, these courses are usually called "stress courses." The children are taken on a guided imagery trip to a fantasy world. They may be told they have a wise man living inside of them that their parents don't know about. They may be told to pretend they are soaring on a fluffy cotton cloud. They may be told to breathe slowly through imaginary holes in your feet, or to imagine a candle floating in a dark room. These are all examples of complaints we have from all over the country. In New Mexico, parents discovered one of these psychological courses called duso. It included 42 guided fantasy exercises, subliminal messages, and New Age practices. Parents were so upset that they got the New Mexico Senate to pass a resolution demanding the elimination "of mind-altering psychological techniques" from New Mexico schools. The education establishment is fighting this all the way because they do exactly intend to have courses that include "mind-altering psychological techniques." In Oregon parents found a course called "Coping for Kids," which included healing practices, psychoanalysis, hypnosis, and guided imagery. In New Jersey, parents found the schools were using transcendental meditation, and when they were unable to get the schools to stop it, they went to court and, in 1977, a federal district judge held that transcendental meditation is a religious exercise brought here from India and has no place in the public schools. I can tell you, however, that in the other 49 states they haven't heard about that decision, and that TM, as it is called, is used very widely. In West Virginia, the telephone company gave a New Age course for its employees and then sent a flyer to all of its customers using the telephone system bragging that teachers from 20 public schools were taking courses in New Age thinking along with the telephone employees. In Florida, parents were upset about a program called "First Aid Kit," which included deep breathing, yoga, self-hypnosis, relaxation, imagery, and centering (which is one of the basic New Age techniques). The child is told he has an open space in the middle of his body which is now going to be filled by new energy. This particular Florida course also had a lot of privacy-invading aspects; for example, the child was instructed to "make a list of 20 things in your house, identify whether they are luxuries or necessities, and then name which member of the family brought that into the house."

In Indiana, parents were upset about a course called "Tactics for Thinking." It included guided imagery; the child is told, "Pretend to be a snowflake. What does it feel like to float, to land? Did you feel happy or sad?" In Nebraska, the course was called "Strengthening of Skills;" the child is told to "feel yourself floating away to a place where you have mastery." The child is taught anchoring and centering, and even that he could "unblock himself" by visualizing a magic ring or a magic energy pill. You can imagine that there are parents who don't want their children taught that they can solve their problems with magic. This course also included the affirmations and the chant, which are common to New Age. In Michigan, a guided imagery course was given to seventh graders who were told they could take a mini-vacation by disengaging from reality and living in a fantasy world. In Alabama, children were given relaxation tapes to listen to, in which they could visualize that they could go to a secret place and sit in a white beam of light and get the answers to all their questions from a wise rabbit.

Now these courses come under a lot of different labels; they may be called "stress courses," or "self-esteem courses," or "human potential," or "higher-ordered thinking skills," or "decision-making." But whatever you call them, they are clearly not academic; they are psychological, and they border on some type of pseudo-religion in the classroom.

There's only one type of these psychological courses that has made its way into coverage by the national news media, because most of these issues are local (they're not national). But the one that has made it into the national media is the "Death and Dying" course. The best article on this subject was published in *Atlantic* magazine, and ABC national TV news gave quite a good and fair piece tour with Sam Donaldson presenting it. He took us into these classes of death and dying where children discussed different ways of dying and different ways of committing suicide. He gave us some morbid visuals and showed how the children were taken on field trips to view the funeral parlors, embalming labs and crematoriums. Sam Donaldson interviewed students who had been through these courses and found them very traumatic and also reported on several students from different states who had committed suicide after taking a course in death and dying. Last month, there was an 8-year-old Michigan boy who killed himself after being shown a suicide film in the second grade.

Now this is just a brief bird's eye view of what is going on everywhere in the country in the public schools. What is the recourse of parents and pupils against these abuses? Normally, when parents complain about these abuses, they are greeted with great hostility by the schools. I have to tell you that the typical attitude of school superintendents and principals and often school boards is the public schools have the right to do whatever they want to with your child, and if you don't like it, your option is to take your child out and put him in a private school. I reject that principle. I feel that any child has got a right to be in the public school classroom without having his privacy invaded by having to reveal his private opinions and attitudes, without having to incriminate himself or members of his family for having done some illegal act, without being subjected to psychological treatment or quasi-religious exercises. It is interesting that the Equal Employment

Opportunity Commission has issued a statement telling employees that they can assert their First Amendment rights if employers try to put them through any of these New Age training sessions, which include relaxation and visualization and imagery techniques. But if they're offensive and a Constitutional violation for adults, how much more so for this captive audience of children in the classroom? What are the remedies?

Well one remedy, of course, would be a school board policy, and there are a couple of school boards that have adopted a good policy against privacy-invading techniques. One of them happens to be up here in Montgomery County in Maryland. But that's only one or two out of 15,500 school districts in this country, and most of them are extremely hostile to any parent who wants to talk about it. Another way to proceed is through invoking the Protection of Pupil Rights Amendment—a federal law. It is a great opportunity; it's there, it's already on the books, the regulations are already there. All it needs is to be enforced. Some of the complaints have been sitting there for years without any action by the Department. And a third way is by lawsuits. There are a few lawsuits, and most of those that have gotten to court have been successful.

14

There was a 1973 federal district court case in which the court wrote a splendid opinion about how one of these courses invaded the privacy and other constitutional rights of the student. But most other places have not heard about that, and these psychological courses go on and on.

I would hope that there might be some of you who would want to help parents and pupils enforce their rights, not only under the federal law, but under the Constitution. The schoolchildren of America need a defendant. They need a pro bono lawyer to represent their rights in order to protect their constitutional right to privacy, their Fifth Amendment right against self-incrimination, their First Amendment right against being compelled to be subjected to religious practices in the classroom, and their right to be in the public school classroom without being subjected to psychological treatment.

Thank you very much for listening.

# June 10, 2010
# Dallas, Texas
# How We Made the Republican Party Pro-Life

I will tell you a story I've never told before. It's a happy story with a happy ending. It's the story of how we made the Republican Party pro-life.

I can remember when it wasn't pro-life. In the 1960s and 1970s, the Republican powers that be thought you shouldn't talk about it, and if you did, "choice" was the favored word. When I went to the 1976 Republican National Convention in Kansas City, I was fighting the Equal Rights Amendment. At that time, the Republican Establishment was not only pro-choice, but also pro-Equal Rights Amendment. ERA had been included in the Republican Platform for many years. Presidents Nixon and Ford were supporters of the Equal Rights Amendment. Betty Ford was an ERA activist.

In 1976 in Kansas City, I made an attempt to get ERA out of the Republican Platform, but failed. However, 1976 was the first Republican Convention after *Roe v. Wade*, and I'm very proud that we put into the Platform a plank calling for a constitutional amendment to restore protection of the right to life for unborn children.

The Republican National Convention of 1980 in Detroit was where we were hoping and expecting to nominate Ronald Reagan. As the time for the Convention approached, it became pretty clear that Reagan was going to get the nomination. So the media decided to make the big news my fight to take the Equal Rights Amendment out of the Republican Platform. I thought having ERA in the Platform was an embarrassment to the Republican Party. We made a lot of plans. We had many prominent people against us. The Governor of Michigan and Republican Congressmen were picketing in the streets against us. The media were all against us—it was a big deal in the media. In fact, later on, when I reviewed the ten years of network coverage of the Equal Rights Amendment, 1972 to 1982, fifty percent of the coverage pertained to the 1980 Republican Convention in Detroit.

Changing the Platform meant we had to go through the Committee process. When ERA came up in the Subcommittee to which it was assigned, and we had some very articulate members on that Subcommittee who were members of Eagle Forum and who were successful in getting the Subcommittee to remove ERA from the Republican Platform. It got to be about 6 pm, and I realized it was a long evening between then and the meeting of the full Platform Committee at nine the next morning. I rushed out in the hall and ran into Jimmy Lyons, a wealthy Republican from Houston, and I said, "Jimmy, don't you belong to some club in Houston with privileges here in Detroit where I can take this Subcommittee?" "Oh," he said, "I don't know, but I'll find out." So he disappeared into the phone booth (this was in the era of phone booths). About ten minutes later he came back and said, "I've got you all set up at the Detroit Athletic Club." So I gathered the Subcommittee and told them we were going to have a wonderful dinner at a prestigious location. I took the Subcommittee (about ten people) to the club, and we wined and dined them all evening. I didn't let them leave until 11 pm. Several on the Subcommittee were articulate advocates of our position, and then we also had some flaky ones who just didn't have the nerve to challenge our well-trained Eagles. So I learned later that the chairman of

18

the Platform Committee, Senator John Tower, had spent the evening trying to call up all the Subcommittee members but couldn't reach a single one and so was totally frustrated. The full Platform Committee convened at nine the next morning and approved the Subcommittee's language. So that meant we got ERA out of the Republican Platform.

The co-chairman of the whole Republican National Committee at that time was a liberal RINO named Mary Dent Crisp. She called a news conference and cried real tears for viewing by the press. She said she was leaving the Republican Party over this issue. Then she went out and backed John Anderson, a renegade Illinois Congressman who ran for President in a Third Party trying to defeat Reagan. Fortunately, he didn't succeed in that and we all know that Reagan won.

We achieved our goal in Detroit. It was such a big political and media fight that we had no difficulty putting in a pro-life plank. The RINOs didn't have any more energy left to fight the pro-life battle.

The next Convention was 1984 in Dallas and that was a really, really fun Convention! That's when I got to know better, and work with, Colleen Parro. We had previously been working together with General Dan Graham for High Frontier, plus some other issues. In 1984, we wanted to make sure that we beefed up the pro-life plank in the Republican Platform. I've been a delegate at most Republican Conventions since 1952, and one of my life goals was to be elected to serve on the Platform Committee. I ran for the Platform in the 1970s and I remember the day when Illinois Senator Chuck Percy stood up in front of all the Illinois Delegates and said, "Phyllis Schlafly is too conservative to represent the State of Illinois on the Platform Committee." Well, by 1984, things had changed: Percy was gone, and I was elected to the Platform Committee. My good friend and skilled politician Kathleen Sullivan arranged that Henry Hyde and I would be elected as the Illinois representatives on the Platform Committee. In 1984 in Dallas we put in the really strong language that we have stuck with ever since. It says, "The unborn child has a fundamental, individual right to life which cannot be infringed." The Platform language also supported a pro-life constitutional amendment and opposed any funding of abortion. We fought for that same language, without changing a comma, ever since because we knew that if the Convention voted any change whatsoever, the media would say we had caved in.

We had a great time at the 1984 Convention in Dallas. Colleen Parro put on a fashion show that was a fashion show to end all fashion shows. We had every prominent Republican lady in that fashion show (such as Mrs. Jesse Helms and Mrs. Jack Kemp), and it was a lot of fun.

The next Republican Convention was in New Orleans, in 1988, and we did let the good times roll. Nominating George Bush I for President was not controversial. Eagle Forum hosted another big event—at every Republican National Convention I've organized and put on a big party. In New Orleans we featured Jack Kemp and Phil Gramm, who were important political leaders at that time.

In 1990, the pro-aborts made their move to wipe pro-life out of the Republican Party. All of a sudden, a Republican fundraiser named Ann Stone announced that she had reinvigorated a Planned Parenthood group called "Republicans for Choice" and was going to raise three million dollars to take the pro-life plank out of the Republican Platform. Almost simultaneously, Mary Dent Crisp, who had been under a rock for the previous few years, started another organization with the same goal. Now, this was rather heavy artillery because, of course, they had the media on their side. Conventional wisdom predicted that at the next Convention, which would be in Houston in 1992, the pro-life plank would become history.

At the time those two pro-aborts made their announcement, three of my best members of Eagle Forum happened to be in Chicago attending a meeting: Colleen Parro, Kathleen Sullivan who was the president of Illinois Eagle Forum, and Penny Pullen, who was a state legislator and pro-life leader in the Illinois Legislature. When they heard the news, they went to the phone booth (we're still in phone booth era), called me up and said, "We have to do something!" "Well," I said, "we've got lots of pro-life organizations; they can take care of this problem."

I then called up all the national pro-life organizations and asked them if they were going to take on this project of stopping these prominent women, who had the support of the media, from taking the pro-life plank out of the Platform. And they all said no, because they wanted to be nonpartisan. Well, I wasn't nonpartisan at all because I believe that the Republican Party is the vehicle for the good things we want for this country, and I've been a Delegate so many times. So the bottom line was, "Phyllis, you have to do it." That is when Colleen Parro and I started Republican National Coalition for Life.

To get started, I had a special luncheon at a top-scale hotel in Washington with several people we wanted to join our effort: Beverly LaHaye; Gary Bauer; and a couple major donors I was hoping would finance this. I had solemnly warned the hotel that one of these big donors was a vegetarian, so make sure he is given a nice vegetarian plate. In the middle of my impassioned speech to get support for our new organization, the waiter walks in with a big plate with nothing on it but twelve long sprigs of broccoli arranged like a clock and one carrot in the middle. I really got thrown in the middle of my speech. But we survived that, and started on our way.

We knew the big fight would be at the Republican National Convention in Houston in 1992; that's where George Bush 41 was up for re-nomination. He was falling in the polls and squishing on life, and the pro-aborts saw their chance. Colleen and some of the rest of us organized our strategy. We wanted to get all the public officials we could to sign a pledge that they would support the pro-life plank, and we started collecting thousands of these signed statements. I remember the night I got Newt Gingrich to sign it; his staff was snarling at me. Nevertheless, we got all kinds of prominent Republicans to sign our pledge. We packaged the pledges in boxes separately for each of the fifty states.

We decided we had to make a splash at the Republican Convention, so we decided that our insignia would be red cowboy hats. We had five thousand red cowboy hats delivered to Susan Feltman's living room in Houston (she was our contact in Houston). We passed them out to the Convention Delegates and they loved them. We were very tolerant; we let people, even if they weren't pro-life, wear our red hats because they looked so big on television; it looked like everybody was wearing the pro-life red hat. We staged a press conference with a lot of attractive girls and these fifty state boxes full of pledges. At the appropriate time in the press conference, we rolled out a long stream of signatures from public officials.

We played the media game, too. We were getting about as much media as the pro-aborts. Since I've had a party at every Republican National Convention, we planned the Houston party for RNC/Life. We got Rush Limbaugh to be our star speaker. Our smashingly successful event was at the Houston Civic Center—a sell-out crowd—with a few other assorted dignitaries like Jerry Falwell and Dan Quayle. And the bottom line is that we kept the pro-life plank in the Platform in 1992.

I don't know what happened to Mary Dent Crisp after that, but Ann Stone kept at her pro-abort project and tried again at the next Republican Convention in 1996, which was in San Diego. At that Convention, I was a Pat Buchanan delegate, and the establishment candidate was Bob Dole. Colleen and I went to San Diego ahead of time to stake out what we needed for our strategy and plans at the Convention. First, we needed a headquarters. I don't know if you realize it, but long before a Republican National Convention meets, the National Committee locks up all the venues, all the hotels, and all the places where you can have parties so that the Party controls everything in the city. We were able to find a little small hotel right smack across from the Convention Center that was in bankruptcy, so it hadn't made it onto the Party's list. That's where we had our headquarters, and Pat Buchanan and Gary Bauer were then able to set up their headquarters there, too. We chose white cowboy hats for our RNC/Life insignia.

Meanwhile, the pro-aborts were working very hard at least to water down the pro-life plank if they couldn't eliminate it altogether. 1996 was the year when Arlen Specter ran for President. When he announced his candidacy for President, his number-one plank was that he was going to get rid of the pro-life plank in the Republican Platform. California Governor Pete Wilson did the same thing; he had just been reelected Governor of California with a larger majority than Reagan ever received, and Wilson was riding high. He announced he was running for President and that his number one plank was to take the pro-life plank out of the Republican Platform. So we had heavy artillery against us. Again, we mapped our strategy. Colleen traveled around to many State Republican Conventions, got them all keyed up to the battle, and encouraged them to elect the right people to the Platform Committee.

Of course, we wanted to have a party again, and what's the biggest thing in San Diego? It's the whale, of course. So I went to Sea World and made a deal for our party. I was fortunate to sign the contract just thirty minutes before the RNC discovered it. Our party at Sea World again attracted a thousand people and was another big success. My party during the Republican National Convention is always the biggest non-official party of the week and the most fun.

Bob Dole was steadily moving toward his nomination for President. The chairman of the Platform Committee that year happened to be Henry Hyde. At every Convention, we in RNC/Life identified our true friends on the Platform Committee. We would always have a little secret caucus ahead of time to plan what we were going to do and give our friends their assignments. In San Diego, we had our dinner caucus in a restaurant where we had to climb about two flights of steps to get there, making sure that nobody could find us.

Henry Hyde, as you all know, is one of the great leaders of the pro-life cause. He had done so many wonderful things for pro-life and he was an articulate speaker. But like everybody else, he had one defect, and his defect was that he was a long-time, good buddy-buddy of Bob Dole. So he didn't want to do anything to hurt Bob Dole. Bob Dole was always very difficult to deal with. He wanted to get rid of the pro-life plank because we're still in the era when the Republican establishment considered it a no-no to talk about abortion. His "Plan B" was to put additional language in the Platform about tolerance. We didn't want to say we're tolerant of abortion; that just wasn't on our agenda at all.

We had our secret meeting upstairs over this little restaurant, and I invited Henry, who was a longtime, personal friend, to come. He came. I introduced him, and we then called on each Delegate around the table to have his or her say about the pro-life plank. We got halfway around the table, and Henry Hyde couldn't take it any longer; he got up and walked out. He realized that we were an "immovable rock"—we were not going to change; we were not going to allow any tolerance language to be put in.

Meanwhile, we were also working with Bob Dole's staff. Dole was calling them all the time, telling them what he was demanding. Finally, his own staff pulled the telephone plug out of the wall so they couldn't hear from him any more. And then, when he met the press, he said he hadn't read the Platform and wasn't going to pay attention to it anyway. But despite all obstacles, we won again, and the Platform was unchanged.

The next Convention was in 2000 in Philadelphia. Again, we had a fabulous party; it was at the Philadelphia Union League Club and was another great success. The bitter feminists were picketing outside the Union League Club, but they didn't bother us. We gave vests to all the pro-life Delegates that said "The *Life* of the Party." That became our slogan; it proclaimed that the pro-lifers are "the life of the party." So we had our "life of the party" party. And it was again a big success.

In 2004 the Republican National Convention was in New York City. By this time, it was becoming conventional wisdom that the establishment had better not try to remove the pro-life plank, because we were determined to keep the plank as it always was. We liked the language we had, and we didn't want it muddied up or watered down. We hosted our fabulous party at the Tavern on the Green featuring Ann Coulter and other valiant pro-lifers to whom we gave awards.

By the time we got to St. Paul, Minnesota, in 2008, it wasn't a big battle any more. The pro-aborts gave up fighting us. We have established that the Republican Party is *the* pro-life Party. It is now really very difficult for anybody to get a

Republican nomination that doesn't at least say he's pro-life. They may not be as totally pro-life as we are, but now nearly all Republican candidates like to say they're pro-life. RNC/Life has a very detailed questionnaire that candidates are asked to fill out so we find out what they really stand for.

We're not only winning in the Republican Party; we're winning nationwide. The polls now show that the majority of people want to say they're pro-life. It's so great to be with people who care about politics, because I think that's where the action is; and that's where the fun is. You need to be part of the action. It's through the Republican Party that we have been able to achieve pro-life goals. The whole country is coming our way; I am particularly cheered when I talk to young people. If you look at the polls carefully, you will find that the young people are more pro-life than the older people. It's very important that we keep on nominating candidates who are pro-life and will vote pro-life and stick with us on the related issues, such as the healthcare bill and the confirmation of judges.

So it's been a tremendous fight. Colleen did most of the tedious work, and I just put my name at the top of the page so you'd know that Eagle Forum is really pro-life. Colleen did all the tiresome work of making those thousands of phone calls, going to all those boring caucuses, sitting through all those tiresome meetings, and confronting all those public officials and making them fill out the questionnaires. It's kind of like bringing up children, you know; you have a lot of repetitious drudgery and at the end, you've got something worthwhile to show for it. We've really got something big and important to show for all that drudgery, and we thank Colleen for her dedication. It's been a tremendous battle; it wouldn't have happened without what she's done, and I want to pay tribute for her wonderful work. We have made the Republican Party pro-life. We have made it essential for Republicans to say they're pro-life. That's the way we're going to win: through the political process.

## January 1, 1975
## St. Paul, Minnesota
## The Equal Rights Amendment (ERA)

There are two contrary views of women in our society today. One is, I think, best demonstrated by an old story that goes like this: They say when men die and go to heaven, they are required to go through one of two doors. On the first door are inscribed the words "Men Who are Dominated by Their Wives." Over the other door, there's "Men Who Dominate Their Wives." And there is always a very long line in front of the first door, and hardly ever any line in front of the second door. But one day, an insignificant-looking man turned up in front of the door that said "Men Who Dominate Their Wives." And one of his friends called over from the other line and said, "Say, Harry, what are you doing standing in front of that door?" And Harry replied, "My wife told me I had to stand in front of that door."

This demonstrates one view of women. There's another view of women which is popularized by the Women's Liberation Movement, and which was most succinctly stated in a commercial which was developed by the National Organization for Women, the principal women's lib group. And it was one of the television spots in many areas, also in newspapers and magazines and services. This commercial shows the picture of a darling, curly-headed child, and the caption over the picture is, "This normal, healthy child was born with a handicap: it was born female." Now that is the starting assumption of the Women's Lib Movement, that somebody—it isn't clear who; maybe God, maybe the establishment, or society, or a conspiracy of male chauvinist pigs—have dealt women a foul blow by making us female, and it is up to legislation or our constitutional amendments to remedy this terrible injustice. And that has been a frame of reference in the way they start.

And so they proposed the Equal Rights Amendment to the Constitution as this remedy for centuries of injustice to women. The proponents of the Equal Rights Amendment go around the country giving us a tiresome litany of past injustices that this world can remedy. They cry out about women not having the right to vote, and women not being able to serve on a jury, and women not being able to go to law school or medical school, and other obsolete things that have long since passed in our society. I really think you have to have psychological problems or have a chip on your shoulder because of what time in this country women have had the right to vote; it's been more than fifty years since this problem was solved. I think the Equal Rights Amendment was very well summed up at the Virginia legislative hearing, by a woman who identified herself as ninety-three years old and a suffragette who had been campaigning for women's rights for more than half a century. She said the proponents of the Equal Rights Amendment are fifty years behind the times; they are fighting a battle that has been long since won. And I think she said it very well, because all these things that they've criticized have long since been passed in our society. Yet they keep talking about it and crying about it. They simply are not relevant to the world that we live in today.

I debated one PhD from the University of Wisconsin who started her talk by saying, "Our sisters in other lands have made more progress toward women's rights than we have in the United States." I said, "Please name one other country

where women are as well off as they are in the United States."
And she had no reply. And yet, supporters of the Equal Rights
Amendment go about saying, "Women in this country are kept
in serfdom. They are treated like cattle. They are second-class
citizens. They are statistically a non-person." This simply isn't
true, and those are not exaggerated statements; those are all
actual quotes from proponents of the Equal Rights
Amendment.

Now, if you were to attend the state legislation hearings
around the country, (as I have been to a number of them), the
first thing that will strike you when you listen to the arguments
of the proponents is that they have no case. They are not able to
cite any injustices against women that ERA will remedy; they
are not able to cite any laws discriminating against women that
ERA will wipe out; they are not able to cite any rights or
benefits that ERA will give them. Many people who have
supported the Equal Rights Amendment in good faith have
done so because somehow they identify it with the slogan
"equal pay for equal work." Now that's a good objective
anybody would support; I did not encounter one person who
was against equal pay for equal work. But the thing you find
out when you listen to the lawyers for the proponents is that

ERA has absolutely nothing to do with equal pay for equal work. As a matter of fact, there is absolutely no way that the Equal Rights Amendment will benefit women in the area of employment. As a matter of fact, when I made that last statement in a debate with Congresswoman Martha Griffiths, who is the leading congressional proponent, she replied, "I never claimed it would."

Now they've closed their case, because most people who have supported ERA have done so because they thought it would benefit women in the area where everyone knows there has been discrimination in the past. But it will not, and every lawyer who has appeared at the state legislative hearings has admitted that ERA will not benefit women at all in the business of employment. ERA doesn't apply to private industry; it only applies to federal and state laws. And the second reason is that there's no way it can consider the effect of the Equal Employment Opportunity Act of 1972. Although this is very specific, it applies to power and fame and emotion. It sets up the enforcing mechanism, the agency that handles the complaints. If any woman thinks she has been discriminated against, she can file her claim; it won't cost her any money; she won't have to hire a lawyer

36

When the women won a $30 million settlement against U.S. Steel, the company was mandated to hire twenty percent women in its production. Now, you may or may not think that hiring women in production in steel mills is an advance in the cause of women but, at any event, those jobs are there if she wants them. And the Equal Rights Amendment will add absolutely nothing to it. And it is a measure of the hypocrisy and the fraud of the Equal Rights Amendment that proponents continue to go about speaking to uninformed groups, and the way they have garbled the law and identify ERA with equal pay for equal work, while their lawyers are supposed to admit and do admit at the state legislative hearings that ERA will do absolutely nothing for women in that area.

Now let's take the matter of education. ERA will do nothing whatever for women in the field of education but the fact of the Education Amendments of 1972. Here again we have a very old law. It applies to different parts of magnet schools, any school that has any federal aid whatsoever covering additions, hiring, promotions, scholarships, grants of all kinds. Well, there's no way that ERA could add anything to women's opportunity to get an education. Now there is an exception to the education amendments of 1972; they exempted admissions to single-sex colleges if they have been traditionally single-sex for many years. Now, there were a number of colleges that actually preferred to retain their single-sex status. We could name a few—Smith, Wellesley, Bryn Mawr, Mount Holyoke—a bunch of exemptions that, of course, would not be constitutional if ERA were ratified. It can exempt any present aid or scholarship grant of any kind whatsoever. And this, of course, would apply to possibly ninety percent of the colleges. You see, a single-sex college by definition discriminates on the basis of sex: a girls' college discriminates against boys, and a boys' college discriminates against girls. Now, what the ERA proponent lawyers will tell you, ERA will end single-sex colleges, and they want it to. They do not feel that one should have the right to make a single-sex college that would discriminate on the basis of sex. Now, I know that most of the people of our day seem to prefer co-ed colleges. I don't see how this advances the cause for anybody to deny those who prefer single-sex colleges their right to attend. But that is the understandable result of ERA that cannot be disputed. Now, when Congress passed the Education Amendments of 1972, it fell to the Department of Health, Education and Welfare for implementation, and it took HEW two years to produce their regulations to implement it.

And so in June 1974, HEW came out with eighty pages of regulations. And there was quite an explosion when they came out, because these regulations said that all sex education classes had to be co-ed, that all gym classes had to be co-ed, and that fraternities and sororities could not continue to operate as single-sex organizations on the campus of any college that received any general revenue. Well, there was quite an explosion, and Jasper Weinberger held a press conference within a week, and said, "I can't exempt the rest of us without specific authority from Congress because I believe that the law requires us to make all these things co-ed."

So then, the Congressmen began to hear from the fraternities and sororities and gym directors that they began to impact through HEW regulations. And then the proponents of the Education Amendments of 1972 threw up their hands and said, "Oh, we didn't mean this when we passed that law!" But, HEW thought it did. So, the Congressmen proposed a draft of a rather quickie amendment, and they got it through both Houses in record speed; it passed just before Christmas, and it specifically exempted from the Education Amendments of 1972 as related to HEW regulations: gym classes, fraternities, sororities, Girls Scouts, Boy Scouts, YWCA, YMCA, boys' clubs, and girls' clubs. And there was no problem; nobody really wanted to wipe out the single-sex nature of these organizations, and that took care of the problem for the time being. Of course, we can certainly recognize such an exemption would become unconstitutional under ERA. If you have a constitutional amendment, you are stuck with it, all over the nation and you've got to take it all down the line in all of these aspects.

Now we see another variation of this in the matter of college and school athletics. HEW has been regulating with the athletic implementation of this Act, and they have now come forth with some regulations. And you may or may not agree with the specifics of it, but they apply what some people might consider a rational approach to the problem. They address women's athletics and say they can compete in non-contact sports, the women have the right to compete with the men. But they do make the provision that, in contact sports, no college or high school is compelled to put girls and boys on the same team.

Now, that type of rational approach is possible at the present time, but now contrast that with what you get under the

Equal Rights Amendment. We have a beautiful illustration of that in the state of Pennsylvania, where they have passed a state Equal Rights Amendment and are already beginning to feel the effects. Just a few weeks ago, the Pennsylvania courts handed down a decision on the state Equal Rights Amendment which mandated every high school in the state of Pennsylvania to permit girls and boys to compete and practice together in all contact sports, specifically including football and wrestling. And this was done under the Equal Rights Amendment and it is mandatory under the Equal Rights Amendment. Now, please note that the decision did *not* say that the school has to have a girls' football team and a girls' wrestling team if you have a boys' team; they would have to compete together. And this is the co-ed nature, the gender-free nature, that is required by the Equal Rights Amendment, and we have this perfect example in the state of Pennsylvania of what the Equal Rights Amendment requires. I think that is just a good example of the nonsense and mischief that is invoked when you require everything that is touched by federal law, state law, the educational systems, public funding, or administrative regulations to be absolutely gender-free. It is the default to every question of the law up and down the line.

Now let's move for a moment from the educational institutions that get public aid to the private schools and see what it's like if we add all girls. There was a Supreme Court decision about a year ago that is relevant to this discussion. Internal Revenue handed down a regulation a couple of years ago that said that any school—private school, that is—which discriminated in its admissions on the basis of race cannot tie up a tax-exempt status. Now, the school in question was a private religious school that did not get any federal aid. But, of course, a private school has a benefit which is known as tax exemption. And Internal Revenue said you can't be tax-exempt if you discriminate on the basis of race, and this ruling was upheld by the Supreme Court. Now I don't happen to agree with that school rule, but I want you to consider what this will mean when a similar ruling is applied to discrimination on the basis of sex, implying that it becomes absolutely clear that no private school, even if it takes no federal aid, would be permitted to function as a single-sex school—as an all-girls or all-boys school—because, by their definition, such schools discriminate on the basis of sex. And while there are not too many at the college level, there are many more at the secondary level. And I ask the ERA proponent lawyers if this will be the result, they say, "Yes, it will be the result, and we *want* it to be the result, because we don't think any educational institution should have the right to discriminate on the basis of sex and still hold tax-exempt status." So, if you want to make all educational institutions at every level, private or public, co-ed, mandated co-ed under federal regulation, ERA would surely do that. Then I saw a senator at this particular hearing ask the proponent lawyer the next logical step: if ERA would put this to private schools, what about the churches themselves, which hold tax-exempt status also? And she hesitated, and didn't care to commit herself one way or the other on the effect that ERA would have on the churches.

Well, I think the logic of this is compelling. We know that the women's liberation movement is making a strong rise at the present time against churches that discriminate on the basis of sex. And while we hold discrimination on the basis of sex, some others have called it simply assigning a different role to men and women in their functions honoring family units. The women's lib movement is making a special drive to force the churches to ordain women as clergy. And they are trying to force the women to go into the seminaries, and into theological institutions and to give them financial aid to get them in, and they will lose their tax exemption if they don't do it. Now, this is certainly one of their objectives.

Now, the tough question is that they look upon the Equal Rights Amendment as the Constitutional basis for litigation to achieve that goal. And that is what they'll do, because this judge will give them the means to litigate toward their objective. Now, there are some churches today that are ordaining women, and they're right to do so; I fully support their right to do that if that is their choice. But there are other churches that do not care to ordain women, and I do not feel that we should give to the Internal Revenue the power to withdraw their tax exemption if they do not.

Let's move onto some other issues. First of all, the right to be exempted from the draft. Now we seem to fight in these foreign wars about every ten years—the politicians keep promising peace, but we keep having these wars about every ten years—and all young men aged eighteen have to register for the draft. You know that if you don't register for the draft, you go to jail—several hundred young men went to jail last year because they didn't register—and the most immediate thing that will happen if the Equal Rights Amendment is ratified is that every eighteen-year-old girl will be compelled to sign up, register, get a draft number, be part of the lottery system and be available for call. Now, this is not what the majority of American women want. The way they line up the support of these women's organizations, they'll go into an uninformed women's group, and they will handle this issue like this: they will say, "Oh, you don't think Congress will really draft women, do you?" Or they will say, "*All* of the women will not be drafted." Well, now those are sleazy arguments, that's it. Nobody ever said *all* women will be drafted; obviously, if you're over age and you only have one eye and one leg you're not going to be drafted. I want you to get the hypocrisy of these types of arguments. In the past, Congress has accepted all married men; the ERA would require it to extend to all married women as well. Now, there are a few people in this audience that can remember back to World War II; they know that men up through age thirty-five were drafted and put into combat, and then there's nothing in ERA that says you don't draft married men or married women; all the ERA does, it says you have to treat the sexes equally; and that is, if the national emergencies call for the draft of married men and fathers and the placing them into combat in some South Pacific jungle, then married women and mothers would have to be treated exactly the same. All ERA requires is a quota.

Now, when these ERA proponents come into the legislative hearing they sing a different tune. They don't put out this stuff of, "Oh, you don't think Congress will really draft women, do you?" Oh, no, they don't think they have to say that to the legislators and lawyers there, so they take an entirely different package. They come in and say, "We *want* women drafted and we *want* women put into combat, and we don't think women will get their equal and full rights in our society until they are treated absolutely equally to men. And I heard one legislator ask one of these proponents, "Well, if we draft women, couldn't you give all the women the desk jobs, the safe jobs, and leave the fighting up to the men?" And she replied, "Oh, no, because that would discriminate against women and deprive us of our equal opportunity to win a Congressional Medal of Honor."

Now let's move onto another subject, and that is the takeaway of the rights of the wives. One of the great things about the country we live in is that it is a society that respects the family as the basic unit. And we have many laws at the state and federal level which are designed to hold the family together. Now, maybe there's some better way that civilization will sometime discover for living together in a civilized community, but I don't know what it is, and I would like to stick with the family as the basic unit.

Now, what laws reflect as an assumption of our society is that the family is what we want for our basic unit. They also reflect the obvious fact that women have babies and men don't have babies. Now I've had some colleges, they tell me they're working on some other alternatives to that, too, but until I see it, I will also start with that as the fundamental assumption. Now take some of these fundamental assumptions: the laws of every one of our fifty states make it a financial obligation of the husband to support his wife. These are good laws; these are laws designed to keep the family together, laws designed to give the wife the right to be in her home with her own babies because we look upon the fundamental home as a good that we want to protect and encourage. These laws also require the husband to provide a home for his wife in accordance with his pay. These laws and other laws require the husband to be the primary support of his minor children. There are many things that these laws reflect in our legal system. This assumption that the husband has the obligation of support is what enables a married woman who does not have paid employment to take benefits in her husband's name. Why? Because the family is what gives her the right to collect against her husband. These are the laws which enables a woman who has made her career in the home to get social security benefits based on her husband's earnings. Why? Because we recognized this obligation before.

Now, these laws of family and family property vary slightly from state to state; there are a number of states that have certain special and unique privileges and exceptions for widows, because we think of widows as a certain class of people who are entitled to some special financial advantage, and these laws vary from state to state, but they're good laws. Now, when ERA comes along, what ERA does is to make everything equal; no matter what the laws say to do, they've got to treat men and women absolutely equally. And this is the takeaway of the rights that the wife now has. In every incident, it will take away the rights that the wife now has; this is why a U.S. Senator called ERA "the most destructive piece of legislation that has ever passed the United States Congress."

Colorado's ERA had already gone into effect. The first thing that happened in this area was that the Colorado court threw out the family support laws – they said that only husbands could go to jail for not supporting their wives; wives can't go to jail for not supporting their husbands, so that's discriminatory, and they struck it down. And then the Colorado legislature addressed itself to the problem, and they did. What will they require under ERA? And that is, they struck out the sexist words – now the sexist words are "male," "female," "man," "woman," "husband," and "wife" – and they replaced them with sex-neutral words which are "person" and "spouse." So now the Colorado law names the principle support "spouse." And anybody can plainly see that's not the same thing at all as saying that a husband will support his wife. So now the wife has an equal financial obligation under pain of being convicted as guilty of a class-five felony. So there is a clause, with normal exceptions made for the wife who is pregnant, or has six children at home, or whatever. It's equality and has to be determined equally.

Pennsylvania's another state with a state ERA; under that, the Pennsylvania courts invalidated the special rights that wives had for maintenance and for payment of lawyer's fees.

They said, "That's discriminatory, let's slow radically down, so we should strike them down." Please know they did not extend it to the men, they just struck them down.

The Pennsylvania courts have also invalidated the Pennsylvania law making the father the primary supporter of his minor children; they put the equal financial burden on all the mothers. Now this is equality, and in no way can you say that this is an advance on the cause of women; it takes away the rights that women now have.

I personally think that if ERA were ratified the ones who will be hurt the most are the senior women – the women who have made being a wife and mother their full-time career, and now no-fault divorce has become rather easy, and if her husband says, "Trade her in for a new model" – she now is being faced with the courts increasingly saying, "This is the age of equality; go out and take care of yourself now." And that is what it is doing to the marriage contract and it is very hurtful to the best interests of women.

Another area it will affect is the area of women and their right to protective labor legislation in the manual labor theater. Now I believe that in professional, academic, or business pursuits, a woman has completely equal labor demands because she's just as smart. But in physical labor a woman cannot compete equally with a man, and it is very unfair to her to put her in a position where the company can push her exactly like a man. It's in recognition of the obvious physical differences between men and women that the state has erected this fabric of protective labor legislation. These are meaningful laws to the women who have nothing to sell in the marketplace but their physical labor. These women don't have careers; they just have jobs, and they're working just because they need the money. And what ERA does is to wipe out the protection that we have formally given them in terms of making them subject to be worked too many hours a day, too many days of the week. Protective labor legislation has mandated certain rest areas, rest periods, chairs to sit down on, sometimes more generous workers' compensation for injuries to more parts of the body for a woman than a man – and these are things that are meaningful to the woman who does manual work. And don't let anyone tell you that when the courts look at this, they will extend them to the men. That is ridiculous, and has not happened in any single incidence. In every case where the protective labor legislation has been struck down under the Civil Rights Act of 1964, the women have lost it and the men have not gained it.

Now, there are all kinds of additional endless mischief and nonsense the ERA is going to cause, and I came upon one recently that I think illustrates this. There was a financial commentator, a columnist, named Sylvia Porter, whose column appeared in the newspapers across the country – I don't know if she appears here, but she's very well-respected as a syndicated columnist in *Money Matters*. She recently said in one of her columns that there was a bill before Congress to require husbands to pay social security taxes on their wives who were in the home and did not have paid employment. And she said, in some length to argue, that this would require the husbands to pay double social security taxes, and that is true; it would be double. But after all, if you have to hire somebody to do the housework, you would have to pay social security on her; therefore, it's only right that he would have to pay social security taxes on his wife. Now, in the words of Senator Sanders, "Whether or not this bill passes, the Equal Rights Amendment, when ratified, will require it."

Now, just think over what this means. I have seen a wide range of estimates as to what the worth of a housewife is; they all started about $12,000 a year and go up. Now it's unclear whether the husband is going to have to pay social security taxes on his wife at the eight percent rate of self-employed persons or at a 5.6 percent rate of people you employ plus an additional 5.6 percent paid by the husband as the employer. But in any event, it would probably figure out to about $960 per year in additional taxes that the husband would have to pay on his wife who does not have paid employment. And, of course, with this additional tax, he will not get any additional benefits because the wife already has the right to draw Social Security benefits based on her husband's earnings. So, if anyone tells you that ERA is going to give new dignity to the housewife, just remember that this "new dignity" is going to cost you those $960 per year in additional taxes. And there are more accounts of people in our country today that are already paid for with social security taxes than they are with income taxes.

Another aspect of the Equal Rights Amendment is Section II. Section II says Congress will have the power to enforce it by appropriate legislation. This is the grab for power at the federal level. This is what they'll take off the hands of the state legislatures, make new areas of jurisdiction that the federal government hasn't yet got its meddling fingers into, including marriage, marriage private law, divorce and child custody – at any time in the legislation, it makes a difference between men and women. Why anybody would want to give a whole batch of jurisdiction to the federal government when it can't begin to solve the problems we have now is more than I can understand. I can't think of the reason why we can find so many people on the federal payroll who are working, lobbying, scraping, and testifying in behalf of the Equal Rights Amendment. They have been doing it for years on your tax money. Time and again, when I go out to speak at hearings, I have to pay my plane fare. I chide my opponents as they spend your tax money. They testify before state legislatures for biddings, they do television debates, they travel all around the country speaking to organizations, they use the telephone calling all over the country. They hold lengthy sessions for employees on government time to tell them why they ought to support the Equal Rights Amendment. Those who are for the Equal Rights Amendment are not for equal rights. They have to get ready all these expensive booklets at taxpayers' expense – they only come out in Washington – and they have all this money to spend; and in the division of money they have many other sources; you know they hire the top political consulting firms in the country to push ERA in the states that have not yet ratified it. They have other sources, too; the Rockefeller Foundation gave $288,000 to the Status of Women Council in California, which was announced to be used for ERA nationally. And millions of dollars from the *Playboy* magazine – this is what happened in the ERA efforts. This is another example of the hypocrisy of the proponents; they try to take the position that they're against people treating women as sex objects like the *Playboy* magazine, but they certainly are quite willing to take *Playboy* money under the table. This is just one more example of the hypocrisy and the difference in the message that the proponents give depending on which type of group they are talking to; you get more truth when you get them at a state legislative hearing when they have to be subject to cross examination.

So here are a couple reasons why the momentum is on our side. Last year, the support was 8-3 in our favor; three states ratified, seven states rejected, and one state rescinded its previous ratification. This year, the score is 14-1 in our favor; one ratified, but fourteen state legislatures rejected the Equal

Rights Amendment. The momentum is all against the Equal Rights Amendment and what it will do, they recognize that. But on the other hand, it is a big takeaway of the rights we now have, and they are coming out in droves in state after state asking the legislatures to rescind their previous ratification and to reject them in the states that have not yet ratified.

Thank you very much.

## September 20, 2002
## Washington, DC
## The 20<sup>th</sup> Anniversary of the ERA Defeat

T his year, we are celebrating the twentieth anniversary of the second and final burial of the proposed Equal Rights Amendment to the United States Constitution. I receive a constant stream of calls from reporters and from students who were born too late to know about ERA and are curious as to why such a righteous-sounding Amendment was defeated. Some are reporters trying to cope with the latest press release from NOW, some are high school students participating in a debate, and some are college students writing a PhD dissertation. In this audience tonight are some who fought with me along the ten-year trail of defeating ERA, but every one of you can be proud that you are part of a movement that stood like the Rock of Gibraltar against ERA's massive attack on traditional values, on life, on marriage, on the family, and on the Constitution. It's so important for you to know the history of ERA so you can explain it to the next generation. They will never learn the truth from their social studies textbooks or from libraries, because they are filled with dozens of books by bitter feminists, while anti-feminist books are censored out. It's up to Eagle Forum members to make sure that the true history is recorded and told to young people.

Tonight I'm not going to give you a legal brief on what's wrong with ERA, or the complete history of how it was defeated in so many states by so many dedicated women, many of whom have already passed on to their eternal reward. That will have to wait until I write my book on ERA. Tonight I'm going to give you a personal view of what the battle looked like from my kitchen, taking you along the campaign trail I traveled for ten years in opposition to ERA.

In the fall of 1971, my priority interest was the danger to America from the Soviet Union continuing to build what we now call weapons of mass destruction. I had written two books on the subject with Admiral Chester Ward, *The Gravediggers* and *Strike from Space*, and in 1971 I was giving a speech all over the country entitled "Evidence of the Soviet Threat," setting forth the alarming facts about the growing Soviet superiority in missiles, megatonnage, and throw weight.

In December of 1971, I received a phone call from a woman I knew only as a purchaser of many copies of *A Choice Not an Echo*. She asked me to come and debate the Equal Rights Amendment in Darien, Connecticut, at a library called The Source. I told her I didn't want to debate anything except the Soviet Threat and, anyway, I didn't know anything about ERA, and wasn't sure which side I'd be on. She replied, "I'll send you a packet of materials and I know which side you will be on."

She was right, and talked me into coming. When Ann Coulter published her bestselling book *Slander* this year, she revealed the coincidence that her brother was on the panel of high school students asking me questions on that memorable evening, December 8, 1971, in Darien, Connecticut, my first debate on ERA. I had started my *Phyllis Schlafly Report* in 1967, and sold subscriptions at five dollars a year. I used the research for my Connecticut debate to write my February 1972 *Phyllis Schlafly Report*, called "What's Wrong with Equal Rights for Women?" I had been writing about nuclear missiles, but that *Report* was the missile that started our movement. The ERA was passed by Congress the next month on March 22, 1979. All news reporters infuriatingly and consistently called

ERA the "Equal Rights for Women Amendment," something
to give "women" equal rights. Of course, ERA does not
mention women; the word is "sex."

> [Sound clip] *The House today by the overwhelming vote*
> *of 354 to 23 passed a proposed constitutional*
> *amendment to guarantee equal rights for women. In*
> *other news, in a historic decision, the Senate voted 84-8*
> *to approve a constitutional amendment guaranteeing*
> *equal rights to women. The proposal goes to the states*
> *for ratification.*

And that's the way it was from the start. A few weeks
later I received an excited 8 a.m. phone call from Ann
Patterson in Oklahoma who said, "Phyllis, we took your *Report*
to the state capitol, and we defeated ERA. Then one of my
*Choice Not an Echo* friends, Marjorie Thoreau in Illinois,
started calling Phil Donahue, whose daily program originating
in Dayton, Ohio, was attracting a national following. She
nagged and nagged his producer to invite an obscure housewife
from a little river town in Illinois to balance the several
feminists he had featured on his program. She finally
succeeded, and I went to Dayton in April, where I shocked

Donahue by making the first national frontal attack on the then-apparently-popular Women's Liberation Movement.

[Sound clip] *Phil: Your daughter, then, is not going to be, sort of, trapped in a house.*

*Phyllis: Well, the house isn't trapping. Are you trying to tell me that it's "liberation" for a woman to go out and sit at a typewriter all day, or stand at a factory machine all day, instead of being in her own home where she can plan her own hours? You know, Phil, the Army has some new ads, some new billboards, out around, and the big headline says the Army has openings for cooks, and then they show a man and a woman standing in front of a big stack of potatoes in an Army kitchen. Now you're going to tell me it's "liberation" for a woman to leave her nice kitchen, with her stove and her sink and her refrigerator that her ever-loving husband bought for her, and go out and cook in an army kitchen and peel potatoes under the direction of some sergeant (and perish the thought if the sergeant is a woman!), and you tell me that's liberation? Why, that isn't liberation; liberation is in the home.*

Well, you missed the punch line: the punch line was: "Perish the thought if the sergeant is a woman!" Well, that show brought a ton of letters from women all over the country who were waiting for someone to refute the feminists. The Illinois State Legislature scheduled a House hearing for June 6. I felt too inadequate to testify about the U.S. Constitution, so I persuaded my attorney husband, Fred, to be our lead witness, and took a carload of my local Republican women friends to the state capitol to support him. Then I began to be invited to debate ERA.

In August, I was on the *NBC Today* show with Barbara Walters; the interview ended with Barbara trying to shut me up with her hands, a memorable TV image that people laughed about all over the country. After that, I realized we needed organized resistance to the ERA steamroller; I invited one hundred women from thirty states to meet me in St. Louis on September 26, 1972. At the Airport Marriott Hotel, we spent all day developing arguments against the ERA; we adopted the name "Stop ERA," and we selected our insignia, the stop sign.

Then the one hundred women and I rode a bus down to the St. Louis riverfront, where we dined on the Goldenrod Showboat. After dinner, I climbed up on the stage where so many melodramas had been performed, just like in the famous musical *Showboat*, and I gave a speech on leadership. I didn't just ask them to defeat ERA; I urged those girls—that's what we called ourselves in those days—to go home and become leaders in the cause of good government, to set up a statewide committee to stop ERA, and, paraphrasing the title of my first book, to be a voice, not an echo. Then Anne McGraw sang one of my favorite songs, "Stout-Hearted Men." Little did we know that night how stout-hearted we would have to be over the next ten years.

Well, that was the start of a David and Goliath constitutional battle waged in state capitols across America. When Congress sent ERA to the states, it looked unstoppable. It had the "big mo," that is, political momentum. It had such a good name; who could possibly oppose equal rights? Supporting the ERA were all members of Congress except eight in the Senate and twenty-three in the House, all the pushy, prominent women's organizations, a consortium of thirty-five women's magazines, numerous Hollywood celebrities, ninety-nine percent of the media, everybody who had pretentions to power in politics from left to right (that is, from Ted Kennedy to George Wallace), and three Presidents of the United States: Richard Nixon, Gerald Ford, and Jimmy Carter.

[Sound clips] *President Nixon said today that he favors passage of the Equal Rights Amendment for Women. / The Equal Rights Amendment, which I wholeheartedly endorse, has not yet been ratified by the number of states necessary to make it a part of our Constitution. Let 1975, International Women's Year, be the year that ERA is ratified. / Vice President Mondale today called the Florida state legislators at President Carter's request urging support of the Equal Rights Amendment. It comes up for a senate vote there tomorrow. The National Organization for Women has threatened an economic boycott of Florida if ERA fails, that boycott to include persuading organizations to cancel conventions there.*

But the unstoppable was stopped by the unflappable Stop ERA ladies in red. A little band of women headquartered in my kitchen on the bluffs of the Mississippi River in Alton, Illinois, had fought and defeated all the big guns of modern politics. The first state that made national ERA news was Arkansas, where a hearing was called in January 1973. Even though a majority of legislators were signed on as co-sponsors, friends urged me to fly to Little Rock and testify, and I did. ERA was derailed that day by the spontaneous reaction of Arkansas women.

[Sound clip] *One legislator got fifty letters in a day. The letters and calls came mostly from older, middle income, conservative women. Some were fearful that if the Amendment were passed, women would be drafted. Others imagined radicals were out to make men and women use the same public restrooms. A group from the south of the state chartered a bus to the capitol and made their protests in person. Aside from their specific fears, the women all seemed to share the general deep fear: this Amendment would somehow change their roles as women, and change what might now be expected of them.*

After Arkansas, the calls for me to come to state capitols came fast and furious, and I started a frantic schedule to testify at one state capitol after another where I faced hearing rooms, usually packed with hostile feminists and bewildered state legislators. In February 1973, I testified at hearings in Richmond, Virginia; Jefferson City, Missouri; Atlanta, Georgia; Raleigh, North Carolina; and Phoenix, Arizona. On the way back from Phoenix, I stopped off in Omaha to have breakfast with Nebraska legislators. The result was that Nebraska was the first state to rescind its ratification of ERA.

From there, I flew to Bismarck, North Dakota, then to Columbia, South Carolina, and then all the way out to Las Vegas, Nevada, where the legislators allowed me exactly four minutes to make my case. All that was in February.

What I did at those hearings was to lay down the strategy of how ERA should be debated. I argued that ERA was a fraud; it would give no benefits to women, but would instead take away legal rights that women then possessed, such as the right of an eighteen-year-old girl to be exempt from the military draft, and the right of a wife to be supported by her husband. We documented our arguments straight from the writings of the pro-ERA legal authorities: Yale Professor Thomas I. Emerson's one-hundred-page article in the *Yale Law Journal* and ACLU lawyer Ruth Bader Ginsburg's book, *Sex Bias in the U.S. Code.* The ERA-ers couldn't show any specific benefits to women, so they spent most of their time attacking me. We never criticized our opponents, but stuck strictly to the legal arguments. Another document we used was *Revolution: Tomorrow is Now,* a publication of the National Organization for Women that set forth NOW's radical pro-abortion and pro-lesbian goals. We reprinted this document and sold it to raise funds for Stop ERA. We told people to be sure and read both sides of the issue.

Then, I went to New York City to appear on the *Mike Douglas Show* against NOW President Wilma Scott Heide. Television in those days was very different; while television coverage was biased against us twenty-to-one, at least there were some programs where I could say a couple of sentences without being cut off. When Mike Douglas introduced me, he said, "Mrs. Schlafly, you have seven minutes to tell us what's wrong with ERA, and Ms. Heide will have the same." Can you imagine Bill O'Reilly or Sean Hannity telling a guest, "You have seven minutes to answer?" Now the guest is lucky to get seven seconds without interruption.

My travels continued. I went twice to Columbus, Ohio, to testify at state legislative hearings, and twice more to Richmond, Virginia and to Charleston, West Virginia. I went to Nashville, Tennessee to testify for rescission. I made my first trip to Florida to debate a loudmouth feminist in Miami. I didn't need to go to Tallahassee because Shirley Spellerberg, who had figured out the evils of the ERA before I did, was effectively lobbying her legislators.

Meanwhile, a powerful pro-ERA push was building in Illinois that we had to deal with. Our little group, then headed by Kate Hoffman, had a brilliant idea; actually, the best idea of our whole ten-year campaign, the idea that the feminists would later call our "dirty trick." We decided to take a loaf of homemade bread to every one of our two hundred, thirty-six Illinois state legislators. We got women all over the state to bring their homemade bread to the motel across the street from the capitol. We borrowed a hotel laundry cart and wheeled it into the capitol and delivered the bread to each office. The next day I got worried that we might have missed a legislator, so I sent a letter to all of them to let me know if they didn't get a loaf. One Chicago representative wrote me right back and said, "You did miss me, and I want my bread. And furthermore, I want banana bread." So we made a special deal of taking him banana bread. He was a young bachelor who didn't care one way or the other about ERA, but he supported us ever after. I testified at two Illinois hearings that year, and ERA was defeated in both the Senate and the House. The pro-ERA-ers began to put me up against their heavyweights. On May 1, I drove to Bloomington, Illinois, to debate Betty Friedan at Illinois State University; that's the day when she famously said she'd like to "burn me at the stake." She said other things that are too indecent to tell in mixed company; since Friedan is not dumb, I assume her purpose was to taunt me into saying something stupid.

I made my first ERA trip to Alabama, where Eunie Smith arranged for me to do a televised debate with a then-prominent feminist, Sissy Farenthold. I did a TV debate with Congresswoman Martha Griffiths and with Pat Schroeder; they never denied my argument that ERA would draft women.

[Sound clip] *Pat: The point is that under the Equal Rights Amendment, Congress will no longer have the option; congress will be constitutionally required to draft women on the same basis as men.*

*Host: Do you agree with that, Congresswoman Schroeder?*

*Pat: I agree that we have the power, and whether or not we will continue to use it depends on the state of emergency.*

*Host: Do you agree that you will have no option if the Equal Rights Amendment passes?*

*Pat: That's right, we'll have to put laws in that apply both to males and females equally, and that—*

*Phyllis: Do you want to draft women?*

*Pat: —and that you can only draft women for combat duty if they can perform the same functions, and men and women would have to be equal.*

*Host: Do you think that's desirable?*

*Pat: Yes, I think that's all right.*

Remember, in 1973 we were just emerging from the Vietnam War, and the draft was not very popular. Every September, we had another Eagle Council with various training sessions on tactics and media. Since we didn't have any paid staff, we rewarded our worthy workers with Eagle Awards.

The year 1974 was more of the same; I traveled to testify at hearings in Augusta, Maine; Montpelier, Vermont, and again in Jefferson City, Missouri; again in Richmond, Virginia, and again in Charleston, West Virginia, and again in Springfield, Illinois. In between, we were making many drives to the Illinois State Capitol to lobby legislators. One of the many television debates I did that year was on Tom Snyder's *Tomorrow Show*. He wanted to stage a couple versus couple debate, and he had a really hard time digging up any pro-ERA leader who had a husband. The only one he could find was Brenda Feigen Fasteau, and we debated on national television.

[Sound clip] *Phyllis: The Equal Rights Amendment would impose a doctrinaire equality on men and women, and that's why we think it is a fraud because it will actually take away from women some of the important rights they now have by law. For example, it will take away women's right to be exempt from the draft and to be exempt from combat duty; it will take away the right of a wife to be supported by her husband in a home provided by her husband and her right to have her husband support her minor children. It will impose an equal obligation on the wife for the financial support of her family. In addition to that, it would wipe out all of the protective labor legislation on the books, which is very necessary and a benefit to working women who work in industry and do manual labor.*

*Tom: All right, Mark; why the ERA, if ratified and put into law, will not put women in combat as suggested by Fred and Phyllis.*

*Mark: First of all, less than a fraction of one percent of men eligible for the draft ever get into what can be called "combat," to begin with. Secondly, the*

*Amendment would require not that women, per se, be put in with men, per se, into combat, but that all physically qualified persons be put into combat without regard to sex. Women are now required, if they want to get into the military, to be better qualified better educated—more character references and so on—and are thus deprived of the extensive and important GI benefits. I mean, they may not be important to the people in your income category, but they are to an awful lot of people, and that's a way in which women suffer, I think.*

*Phyllis: Yet, here are some very important points; now, I can tell you that the lawyers for the Equal Rights Amendment are saying that the height and weight standards and physical requirements would have to be adjusted to reach a mean between men and women.*

*Mark: Which lawyers?*

*Phyllis: Well, such as Dr. Emerson of Yale, who's the leading legal "light" of the proponents; that's his claim in his article. And then, most women are larger than the*

73

*most decorated man in World War II , Audie Murphy. I can tell you that at the Virginia ...*

*Brenda: Most women are larger?*

*Phyllis: Yes, larger than Audie Murphy.*

*Mark: But are they stronger?*

*Fred: He was only 120 pounds; he'd have to eat half a dozen bananas to make 125 pounds to get in the Army.*

*Phyllis: All right.*

*Fred: And he was the most decorated man in World War II, Audie Murphy. Five feet two.*

*Brenda: I don't think it's true that most women are larger than 125 pounds at this moment.*

*Phyllis: All right. Now, at the Virginia hearing, the legislators asked one of the proponents, "Couldn't we give the women ..."*

*Tom: I was going to ask for a weight and height chart here, but I'm not going to do it.*

*Phyllis: ... asked one of the proponents, "Couldn't we give the women the safe jobs and give the men the fighting jobs?" And she replied, "Oh, no, because that would discriminate against women and deprive them of their equal opportunity to win a Congressional Medal of Honor." Now, most Medal of Honor winners are dead. And it isn't true that only one percent go into combat; the latest Pentagon figures were that twenty-two percent were in combat in Vietnam.*

You can see how mad Brenda was! After the debate, she left her husband and went to live with her lesbian girlfriend.

1975 opened up with a bitterly cold trip to testify in Bismarck, North Dakota. I remember that hearing very well, because it was where I heard the one and only example of a state law that discriminated against women that ERA would remedy. In North Dakota, they had an old law still on the books that said that wives could not make homemade wine without their husband's consent.

Then, I testified at another round of state legislative hearings in Carson City, Nevada, twice more in Jefferson City, Missouri, and twice more in Springfield, Illinois. By this time, I was usually arranging to speak last so I could immediately refute the false arguments made by the ERA-ers. On Valentine's Day, I did an exciting debate on ERA before the entire Arkansas Legislature. That was the year when I decided to go to law school in my spare time, so I would be sure never to let our movement down by inaccurate statements.

Then came hearings in Columbia, South Carolina; Providence, Rhode Island; Denver, Colorado, and in Frankfurt, Kentucky, to urge rescission. At most of these hearings, I faced a room full of angry feminists. But one hearing was different; Austin, Texas, was unforgettable because a friendly audience of thousands of women wearing pink dresses came out to support me. Meanwhile, the battle in Illinois was ongoing. I could sense we were falling behind. I would take a few carloads of women to Springfield to lobby every couple of weeks, but I could see we were not having enough of an impact. The odds were so great against us. We had small demonstrations in February, March, April, May, June; Illinois held another vote, and we won, but each vote was getting more scary. At that time, everyone in Illinois had one state senator, two state representatives of one party, and one state representative of the other party. That meant each constituent had to contact four representatives in Springfield. I prepared a flyer with four coupons with the names of the representatives and had five thousand copies printed separately for each district in Illinois. I loaded the immense stack of flyers in my station wagon, drove up the state, making stops all up Illinois, to give them to a Stop ERA-er who would get people to sign and mail them in. The mail then started to pour into Springfield.

In November, we had an unexpected boost to our morale; New York and New Jersey both had a referendum on adopting a state ERA and, contrary to all predictions, both liberal Northeastern states decisively rejected ERA.

1976 started with a trip to Pierre, South Dakota, to rescind that state's ratification of ERA. The successful South Dakota rescission effort was brilliantly managed by Kitty

Werthmann. In February, I led our women into doing something they had never done before, and they were very apprehensive about it. I led a small group of Stop ERA women to picket in front of the White House in Washington to protest Betty Ford's lobbying for ERA.

> [Sound clip] *First Lady Betty Ford has been actively campaigning for the constitutional amendment to provide equal rights for women, even to the point of telephoning state legislators. About thirty-five pickets showed up at the White House today to protest her activity, but Mrs. Ford told reporters she's sticking to her guns.*

A couple of our ladies told me later they confessed to their husbands that they had done something that might have been immoral, but they did it for Phyllis and the cause. Then came April 27, 1976: the day that changed the face of politics forever. Illinois was the frontline of the battle, the state the ERA-ers most wanted to get, and where they had all their big political guns on their side: the governor, the Senate and House leadership, and the media. I realized that our friends in the legislature were intimidated by the razzmatazz of celebrities and media and money and aggressive feminists and, furthermore, they didn't really believe that our side was in significant numbers to matter. Up until that time, ERA had been held back by just a handful of people consisting of a few dozen Republican women who had gone to Washington with me in 1967 to try to elect me president of the National Federation of Republican Women, the local representatives of the National Council of Catholic Women, and one brave Orthodox Jewish rabbi in Chicago. I decided we had to have an event to convince the legislators we were real, and that there were lots of us. I dreamed we could bring a thousand people to our state capitol to rally against ERA, something that had never before happened in our state. Where could we find more troops? Only one place: the churches. So we sent out the message to all the churches: all the Protestants and Evangelicals, the Catholics, the Mormons. The essential player in that first big rally was Eagle Forum's original first vice president, Tottie Ellis, and her husband Carol, a professor in a Church of Christ seminary in Tennessee, who telephoned his ex-students living in Illinois and told them to come to our rally.

And a thousand people came from all over the state, many riding on buses with signs that read "Joy" and "Jesus

Saves." Many carried babies in their arms; we had homemade signs galore. Those were my singing days, and I sang a parody I wrote called "Bella's Bunch." We hand-delivered our homemade bread to all the offices. Somehow, I can't find any press photos to show you of that landmark event, but that thrilling Stop ERA rally in Springfield completely changed politics. That was the day that Eagle Forum invented the pro-family movement, and we all know how it has grown to become a mighty national force. That momentous day in Springfield, Illinois, was a coming together of believers of all denominations, many of whom had never been together before, but whom we persuaded to work together for a political goal we shared; namely, protection of the traditional rights of wives, of eighteen-year-old girls, of marriage and the family, and of the Constitution itself against the radical feminists and their destructive push for a gender-neutral society. That rally morphed our little Stop ERA committee into a mighty movement that the legislators had to deal with.

The ERA-ers, led by NOW, decided they had to respond with a rally of their own, which they staged three weeks later. Indeed, they did put on a big rally, but we were ready for them. We arranged for an airplane to buzz overhead carrying a streamer that read: "Illinois women oppose ERA. Libbers go home." We hired two photographers to take pictures of their rally, which I then published in the *Phyllis Schlafly Report*. A picture tells a thousand words, and those pictures proved that their ranks were filled with lesbians, abortionists, Socialist Worker Party activists, and other unkempt radicals. Illinois was not the only state where ERA-ers displayed their radical streaks. Lee Wei Song will remember how twenty ERA-ers paraded into the Georgia State Capitol in Atlanta dressed in purple pantsuits and wearing bus driver caps that said "Gay and proud of it." We were also helped in Virginia when the ERA-ers spit on the Speaker of the House, staged a sit-down at the state capitol in Richmond, and had to be carried out by police.

> [Sound clip] *The deadline for ratification is March 22, 1979—little more than a year away—and the amendment is still three states short of the necessary thirty-eight. As time grows short, the fight has become increasingly bitter. ERA supporters were arrested after they protested defeat in the committee of the Virginia Legislature.*

The rest of 1976 was taken up with more debates with leading feminists. Over the ten years, I debated every feminist you ever heard of with the exception of Gloria Steinem, who consistently refused to debate me. I debated every president of NOW, Karen DeCrow fifty times, Eleanor Smeal I've lost track of how many times, Patricia Ireland; other feminists I tangled with include Bella Abzug, Betty Friedan, federal bureaucrat Catherine East, congressional sponsors of ERA Martha Griffiths in the House and Birch Bayh in the Senate, Mrs. Birch Bayh, Jill Ruckelshaus, Barbara Mikulski, Melissa Fenwick, Joyce Brothers, Maureen Reagan, and Sarah Weddington of *Roe v. Wade* fame over fifty times.

1976 was the year when I started my long series of college speeches and debates, which now number more than five hundred. In 1977 the hearings started all over again, and I resumed my travels. The ERA-ers forced all the states that had rejected ERA to go through the process again and again, with more hearings and more votes. I testified in Indianapolis, Indiana; Atlanta, Georgia; Topeka, Kansas; and Little Rock, Arkansas. In February, I led a picket line in front of the White House to protest Rosalynn Carter lobbying for ERA.

[Sound clip] *Rosalynn: Time is running out, and we, we just have to get the Equal Rights Amendment ratified; it's too important to just let it drift away.*

That time, the demonstration was a lot of fun, and nobody had any regrets. Our spirits were lifted when Nevada defeated ERA on a statewide referendum in February. Thank you, Janine Hansen. We had a big stop ERA rally in Raleigh, North Carolina, where the famous Watergate Senator Sam Ervin joined me on the platform. And in March, we had another thousand-person Stop ERA rally in Springfield, and the Illinois House voted again to reject ERA. In March, I went to testify again in Columbia, South Carolina, and Vivian Rice will remember this big rally on the capitol steps.

[Sound clip] *Today is the fifth anniversary of ERA's passage by Congress, and so far thirty-five states have ratified it. Three more are needed to make it part of the constitution. Bill Worden has more from Columbia, South Carolina.*

*Bill: It is not a happy birthday for ERA; the motion here in South Carolina is running strongly against it, as it is in all other southern states. When the state Senate began public hearings today, Stop ERA forces topped off a long campaign with a rally on the capitol steps. The national chairman of Stop ERA, Phyllis Schlafly, believes it should never have come this far.*

*Phyllis: The Equal Rights Amendment would be dead today if it were not for the massive federal spending and White House interference that is trying to cram ERA down our throats.*

In April, we had just as exciting a rally in Tallahassee, led by Shirley Spellerberg, who turned out twenty-five hundred people, but ten ERA-ers standing on the other side of the capitol got all the media coverage.

In April, I also went to New York City to receive a reward from the Women's National Republican Club at the Waldorf Astoria; that was the day that the ERA-ers hired a professional pie thrower to hit me in the face with an apple pie.

The Illinois activities went on and on. In April, I had to testify again in Springfield, and we had more rallies. That year, we had an apple pie day, taking a homemade apple pie to all two hundred, thirty-six legislators. That was an exhausting undertaking, but we had to show them that we're "for Mom and apple pie."

In the fall of 1977, our cause looked hopeless. The ERA campaign was run right out of Jimmy Carter's White House in what is called the War Room. Carter's daughter invited legislators in key states to come to the White House to be schmoosed for ERA. I remember one brave Democratic state legislator from Miami who was invited twice to the White House to be lobbied by Carter's daughter to switch from "no" to "yes." That's heavy stuff; a lot of people would do most anything for a White House invitation. But he stood firm, and when the libs realized they couldn't get him to switch, they turned on him viciously. They filled his mail with every kind of obscenity, including a lot of disgusting items I can't even describe to this audience. But he never switched.

In 1977, the ERA-ers knew they needed reinforcements so, like typical liberals, they went to the government for help. They got Congress to appropriate $5 million for a tax-funded lobby for ERA called International Women's Year, known as

IWY. A convention in each of the fifty states elected delegates to go to Houston in November 1977. No opponent of ERA was permitted to speak from the platform in any of those fifty tax-funded meetings or the national convention. The elections were full of fraud and shenanigans to ensure that the feminists had a decisive majority of delegates.

The International Women's Year Convention opened in Houston with Bella Abzug as chairman and three First Ladies sitting with her on the platform: Rosalynn Carter, Betty Ford, and "Lady Bird" Johnson. Among the delegates was every feminist you ever heard of, and they set forth their demands, telling the world what women want, starting with ratification of ERA. Three thousand media people were on hand to give them massive publicity, with wall-to-wall television coverage for their hot button issues: ERA, abortion, and gay rights. Thanks to public television coverage, you have a close up look at the feminists.

> [Sound clip] *Madam Chairperson, I move the adoption of the following resolutions: the Equal Rights Amendment should be ratified. / I would like to ask this body to give the most resounding and urgent vote*

*demanding the ratification of the Equal Rights Amendment within the coming year! Because, otherwise, the enormous expenditure of energy and money and effort that has brought us to this point will be in vain, and these ten years of movement will be in vain. / There is only one thing, get used to this word, and that is Equal Rights Amendment. Everyone stand up and vote yes. / The question arises on the adoption of the resolution: all those in favor would you please rise. / We support the U.S. Supreme Court decisions, which guarantee reproductive freedom to women / The resolution on reproductive freedom is adopted. / Madam Chair, I move the following resolution on sexual preference. Congress, state, and local legislatures should enact legislation to eliminate discrimination on the basis of sexual and affectional preference in areas including, but not limited to, employment, housing, public accommodations, credit, public facilities, government funding in the military. This is a feminist issue because discrimination against women begins at the basis of sexuality. There are double standards: one standard for males, another for females; one standard for heterosexuals, another for homosexuals. And all these double standards in the issue of sexuality work to keep women in their place. Human rights are indivisible, and all women, when we march together in equality, we will march as heterosexuals and homosexuals, minority women and majority women, rich and poor; we will all go together as full human beings.*

A couple of months later, a reporter asked the governor of Missouri, "Governor, are you for ERA?" He replied, "Do you mean the old ERA, or the new ERA? I was for equal pay for equal work, but after those women went down to Houston and got tangled up with the abortionists and the lesbians, I can tell you ERA will never pass in Missouri."

The governor was right; IWY was the turning point in the battle over ERA. By the time IWY was over, we had the proof that the ERA agenda includes tax-funded abortions and gay rights. Since IWY in Houston in 1977, ERA has been voted on about twenty-five times in state legislatures, in committees, in Congress, and in several statewide referenda, and it has never had another victory. The reason I'm telling you this story tonight is that you and I have to make sure that it stays that way.

But the media didn't show the worst of the IWY. Even worse were the displays at the booths in the halls where you could pick up booklets on what lesbians do. These pictures give you a real flavor of the kind of people who attended this feminist convention. These pictures somehow never made it onto the network news, and much of it is too obscene to talk about. One of the official IWY publications was called *A Lesbian Guide*. The most popular buttons worn by these delegates were "A woman without a man is like a fish without a bicycle," and "Mother Nature is a lesbian." We in Eagle Forum originally called ourselves the "alternative to Women's Lib." We knew we had to make the country know that these radicals and lesbians did not speak for women. To counteract this tax-funded IWY atrocity, our Eagle Forum board took another hall in Houston across town called the Astro Arena, and simultaneously set out to urge pro-family men and women to come at their own expense. Lottie Beth Hobbs gave us the name "Pro-Family Rally," and the name stuck. November 19, 1977 was the day the expression "pro-family movement" came into the political vocabulary. Looking back, I don't know how

La Neil Spivy had the nerve to contract for a hall that seated fifteen thousand people; we didn't have taxpayers' money to pay travel expenses, and Houston isn't exactly centrally located. But we knew we had to make a statement against ERA. Shirley Curry went to churches and motivated women to ride twenty hours on a bus, come to our Pro-Family Rally, and then return on the bus without ever going to bed. And the buses came and came and came. It was thrilling to see the thousands of people arriving. We filled the Astro Arena to overflowing. They rode hours and hours on the bus and never went to bed, came to our rally, and rode home again. The *Houston Post* reported that we had an attendance of twenty thousand people in a hall that was built to hold only fifteen thousand. We looked a bit different from the other crowd. I remember Bob Dornan standing on the platform with me and saying, "Look at those exit doors crammed body-to-body with people. The fire marshal must have gone home and figured that God will protect this crowd."

[Sound clip] *Phyllis: In order to have held the line for the last five years against the tremendous odds of White House lobbying, federal government expenditures, prominent people, and big money, we had to have somebody on our side who was more powerful than the President of the United States.*

Of course, our rally didn't get much media coverage, but the publicity the ERA-ers got for their tax-funded IWY showed the world that they are a bunch of anti-family radicals and lesbians who want big brother government to solve their personal problems. IWY media coverage dealt a body blow to the feminist movement.

In 1978, the battle in Illinois heated up even more. We had rallies and demonstrations every month, more speeches, more debates. By now I was carrying my bullhorn to give directions to the crowd. I kept sending out what people called "Phyllis's rotunda letters"—meet me in the rotunda of the Illinois State Capitol on Wednesday at 10 a.m. And we kept thinking of different ways to publicize our message. One day, a preacher rented a monkey suit and joined our demonstration, walking around with a sign that said, "Don't monkey with the Constitution." He almost lost his church over that. But we got good press, and there were more votes and we won them all narrowly.

On June 19, we had another huge, noisy Stop ERA rally at the capitol in Springfield. That was the day I carried the two-step ladder I use in my kitchen to get into my top cabinets, planted it in the center of the rotunda, climbed up on it, and accused President Jimmy Carter of calling Chicago legislators to force them to vote for ERA by threatening a cutoff of federal funds. Some of my friends were nervous about that accusation, but nobody ever denied the truth of it. We then won another narrow victory.

It was not just in Illinois that the Carter Administration was trying to pressure legislators to vote for ERA; he did it in Florida too.

> *[Sound clip] Yes, I've had a letter from the President of the United States; this morning, I had a talk with Vice President Mondale. Weather's fine in Washington; does that cause pressure? It may cause for some, but it doesn't for me. / Lewis voted no.*

All our Illinois votes were by fewer than five-vote margins, some just one- or two-vote margins. We always had to win with a changing mix of conservative and liberal representatives, conservative and liberal Democrats, downstate rural guys, Chicago machine Democrats, and the guys who voted yes but secretly lined up others to vote no. One of our best friends was the AFL-CIO spokesman in our legislature, whose arguments were very different from mine. I remember how I cringed the day he called the ERA-ers "a bunch of brainless, bra-less broads."

The one who kept all these politicians in line was Kathleen Sullivan. We could not have won in Illinois without her extraordinary political smarts. She was somehow able to manage all those different factions in the Illinois legislature.

In 1978, I went to Salt Lake City to meet with the VIPs in the Mormon Church, including Barbara Smith. The help of the Mormons was essential to our cause. I didn't actually meet with Mormon President Ezra Taft Benson, but he sent me letters of support and encouragement.

When ERA was voted out of Congress in March 1972, it was given the specific deadline of seven years. In 1978, the feminists woke up to the fact that they might not get their thirty-eight states by the deadline of March 22, 1979, so they devised a plan to get Congress to vote a time extension. I went to Washington to testify against this and spent all summer lobbying members of Congress. In September, we had a lobby day, and hundreds of members of Eagle Forum came to Washington to lobby against the extension. Public opinion was opposed to this unfair time extension. Political cartoonists had a field day, calling it "three extra innings in a ballgame that was not tied up." But we lost. The crooked extension passed the Senate on October 6. The extension was the most peculiar time period in any piece of legislation in history. Congress gave ERA an additional three years, three months, eight days, and seven hours—just long enough to catch the Illinois legislatures' mandatory adjournment on April 30, 1982. So Illinois actually had to vote every year for 11 years.

It was a raucous day at the U.S. Capitol. After the vote, Ted Kennedy led the feminists out on the grass outside the Capitol, and to the cheering crowd of obnoxious feminists he cried out, "Phyllis Schlafly, where are you now?"

[Sound clip] *Ah, Phyllis Schlafly, where are you now?*

That wasn't really Kennedy's voice; that was Bob Dornan mimicking Kennedy.

The feminists were convinced that the three years would give them plenty of time, and we would be so demoralized by the extension that we would give up. Not on your life; the next Eagle Council, we determined to press on. And at the end of 1978, I received my law degree.

In 1979, we started the same routine all over again. I had to testify again before the Illinois House and Senate Committees and we won again; we also kept rescission efforts alive; I even went to Dover, Delaware. The original seven-year deadline set by Congress for ERA was March 22, 1979. We considered that date the constitutional termination of ERA, and we decided to have a party proclaiming that we had won, that ERA was dead constitutionally. It took a lot of nerve to do that, because the crooked extension had already passed. Would anybody come to our party? Well, one thousand, five hundred did. We packed the ballroom of the Shoreham Hotel in Washington for our gala to celebrate what we called "the end of ERA." Those who were there will never forget that evening. In the middle of our program, the hotel manager came to the

platform to announce that he had received a bomb threat and
we would have to evacuate. Fifteen hundred people trooped out
of the ballroom, went to the restroom and, after the dog sniffed
out the place, amazingly, fifteen hundred people returned for
the rest of the program. We made fun of the women's libbers
and sung some cute parodies that I wrote for the occasion.

For me, the most memorable part of that first burial of
ERA was the hostility of reporters at my news conference,
whose attitude was, "How *dare* you say you've won? How
*dare* you say ERA is dead? You haven't won! You're not
supposed to win, and you're not going to win. ERA *will*
become part of the U.S. Constitution." They repeated the chant
of the ERA-ers: Failure is impossible.

> [Sound clip] *We will not fail; we did not get in this fight
> to lose, and we do not intend to lose. We will ratify the
> Equal Rights Amendment for the United States of
> America.*

The title of our gala, "The End of ERA," was a double
play on words. We knew it wasn't really the end of ERA
because the extension loomed ahead of us. But it was the end

of an era, the era of conservative defeats. In the 1960s and 1970s, conservatives were so used to losing all their political and legislative battles that they never even contemplated the possibility of winning. When we proclaimed that we had beaten ERA, we taught conservatives the lesson that it is possible to win after all. 1979 was truly the end of the era of conservative defeats. One year later, conservatives won a smashing victory with the election of Ronald Reagan as President and a Republican Senate. In 1980, the ERA-ers realized they hadn't won a single state since the extension passed; indeed, since IWY in Houston. They realized what a powerful argument we had in stating that ERA would require the drafting of eighteen-year-old girls. So they devised a two-part plan of action to take this argument away from us. Part one was to get President Carter to propose drafting women immediately; part two was to support a lawsuit to get the U.S. Supreme Court to rule that exempting women was sex-discriminatory under the present Constitution.

Now it would be nice to think that we defeated ERA because we were smarter than the feminists, but sometimes I have to admit that it might have been because they were so dumb. You can imagine that Carter's announcement opened up dozens of interviews for me to tell people what a terrible idea that was. All during January, February, March, and April, I gave a steady stream of interviews and news conferences on Carter's plan to draft women. Congress even held the hearing on it. I gave speeches in Chicago; Washington; Columbia, South Carolina; Greensborough, North Carolina; Michigan, Mississippi, and Kansas. Finally, Speaker Tip O'Neill had to tell Carter it was a dumb idea.

On April 30, I had to testify again in Illinois. To combine this with a demonstration, we organized fifty-nine draft-age girls to come to the hearing, one from each legislative district. The feminists were so nasty to those girls; the ERA-ers tried physically to bar those darling eighteen-year-old girls from entering the hearing room and to make their life miserable after they came in. Just recently, I ran into a beautiful young woman who said to me, "Mrs. Schlafly, I was one of your draft-age girls in Springfield back in 1980." I said, "You remember how ugly they were to all of us?" She said, "Yes; they spit on me."

The ERA-ers had their biggest rally in May in Chicago led by Bella Abzug, Phil Donahue, and Marlo Thomas. But we matched them the following day on May 11, 1980, when the Baptists came out in force to support our cause. We had another memorable, thrilling Stop ERA rally at the state capitol in Springfield, and with the Baptists swelling our ranks, we had a body count of twelve thousand people on the steps of the Illinois Capitol building. Our California Eagles, of course, had been bypassed by the whole ERA fight because California ratified early and never really debated ERA, so they held a fundraiser for us at Disneyland. The next day was important. I met with Ronald Reagan in his Los Angeles office, and he promised me he would never support ERA. He also promised me that he would never appoint Henry Kissinger to any office, and Reagan kept both promises after he became President.

Over the ten-year period, the Illinois state legislature voted a couple of dozen times on ERA and on the rules to bring it to the floor. The most dramatic and decisive vote came on June 18, 1980. NOW President Eleanor Smeal had been practically living at the capitol for a month, and tension was very high. She announced she had the votes to pass ERA, so all the national media showed up in Springfield with their TV cameras. President Jimmy Carter was telephoning Democratic legislators and promising them federal housing projects in their districts if they would vote yes on ERA. Governor James Thompson was phoning Republican legislators and promising them dams, roads, and bridges in their district for a "yes" vote. Mayor Jane Byrne was phoning Chicago legislators and forcing them to vote yes under threat of firing them and their relatives from their city patronage jobs. Democratic legislators who were beholden to the Chicago machine wept openly as they apologized to me for having to vote yes so their relatives wouldn't lose their jobs. Cash bribes were flowing and the media were gloating. Our own vote count showed that we were a couple of votes short, and we were worried. The House debated all afternoon. It was a very dramatic few moments as the votes climbed electronically on the board in front of the House chamber, and then a great shout went up as it became clear we had defeated ERA again. The feminists needed one hundred and seven votes, and they got only one hundred and two.

I was standing in the gallery of the Illinois House when *ABC Nightline* sat Eleanor Smeal in front of the camera and said, "Mrs. Smeal, you said you had the votes. What happened?" She replied, "There is something very powerful against us, and it's certainly isn't people." Smeal didn't know what the power was, but we knew: prayer, and the truth. We had done all we could, and the Lord brought us two votes from Chicago legislators who had never voted our way before.

The following month, I went to Detroit for the 1980 Republican National Convention. Support for ERA had been part of the Republican Platform for many years. We tried to take ERA out of the Platform at the 1976 Convention, but we failed. In 1980, it was do-or-die because we didn't want Ronald Reagan to be embarrassed by having to defend a Platform plank in favor of ERA. The media made ERA the hot Convention issue, covering everything the feminists said and did, such as the street demonstration led by Congresswoman Margaret Heckler and the threats of the Michigan governor.

[Sound clip] *Michigan Governor William Milliken: It would be a serious mistake to abandon this Party's support of the Equal Rights Amendment. If we repudiate our 1976 position, then we would be repudiated by a large segment of America's population, and deservedly so.*

That was 1980, remember. While the ERA-ers were prancing around in front of the TV cameras, we were working quietly in Committee. We had a big victory when the Platform Subcommittee voted to take ERA out of the Platform and got ready to adjourn about 6 p.m. Some of our Subcommittee votes were Eagles who had gotten themselves on the Committee, but some others were very flaky, and I knew the pressure would be intense to get them to renege before morning. I rushed out in the hall and found an old friend who knew his way around town, Jimmy Lyons of Houston. I said, "Jimmy, don't you have some exchange privileges at a club in Detroit where I can take the Subcommittee to dinner?" He said, "I don't know, but let me make a call."

He disappeared into a phone booth and came out a few minutes later with the good news that he had set us up for dinner at the Detroit Athletic Club. I took the whole hungry Subcommittee to the club and wined and dined them all evening. Nobody knew where we were; nobody could reach us by phone. Thank goodness we were in the pre-cell phone era! I learned later that Platform Committee Chairman John Tower spent all evening trying to contact Subcommittee members one by one but never reached anybody.

The full Platform Committee met at 9 a.m. the next morning and approved the deletion of ERA by the stunning vote of 90-9. That was the end of Republican Platform support of ERA.

In 1981, the most important things that happened were two court cases, and we won both of them. The U.S. Supreme Court handed down its decision in the case brought by the feminists and the ACLU to force the military draft to be sex-neutral. The Court ruled in *Roster v. Goldberg* that it is perfectly constitutional for our government to draft men and not women. This was a tremendous victory for girls and for society and for our campaign to stop ERA because it was clear that if ERA were in the constitution, the result would have been the opposite. The other court case involved two issues: whether the crooked time extension voted by Congress to give ERA three extra years was constitutional, and whether the rescissions of ERA by five state legislatures were constitutional. The case was tried in federal district court in Idaho, one of the five rescinding states. The others were Nebraska, Tennessee, Kentucky, and South Dakota. A wonderful judge in Boise gave us a Christmas present on

December 23, ruling that the time extension was illegal because it attempted to change the rules in the middle of the game, and that it is constitutional and okay for a state to change its mind and rescind, so long as it is before an amendment is locked into the Constitution by three-fourths of the states. The ERA-ers appealed this decision to the U.S. Supreme Court, which sat on the case until after the extension time expired in 1982, and then issued a ruling stating that the Court didn't have to decide those issues because ERA was dead regardless of whether it died in 1979 or 1982.

When 1982 opened, everybody sensed we were running the last lap of the race. The ERA-ers announced they had raised $15 million for a television blitz in key states with celebrity endorsements. We knew we would have close votes, and pitched battles in the four most hard-fought states. We knew we had done everything humanly possibly, and we just had to count on the good Lord to do his part too. That's why we had the nerve to plan our second burial of ERA when the time extension ran out on June 30.

On January 19, Oklahoma defeated ERA for the last time, 27-21. On June 4, North Carolina defeated ERA for the last time, 27-23. The pro-ERA-ers then sent bags of chicken droppings to the twenty-three senators who voted no in North Carolina. On June 21st, Florida defeated ERA for the last time, 23-17. Thank you Shirley. The knock-down, drag-out pitched battle was in Illinois. Throughout the spring, we had to keep facing more ERA votes on procedure and rules, and we kept winning. The ERA-ers were getting desperate. In April, the ex-communicated Mormon Sonia Johnson started a hunger strike on the first floor of our state capitol. When the press came to me for a comment, I said I thought that was a good idea, since most of them ought to go on a diet. But after a couple of days, it wasn't funny anymore. The air in the state capitol was so tense you could cut it with a knife. We began to be afraid there might be some kind of collapse or accident, and that a motion would bring about passage. In May, a "chain gang" of pro-ERA-ers chained themselves to the door of the Senate chamber on the third floor. They stayed for weeks; the state police never removed them.

On May 4, we had one more big Stop ERA rally in Springfield, when we had speeches, songs, and delivered our famous homemade bread to every legislator. On June 8, I gave my testimony on ERA to a state legislative hearing for the forty-first time. This time it was in the House chamber with the TV lights glaring. Again, I rebutted the pro-ERA-ers' arguments. This time, my eighteen-year-old daughter Anne was our star speaker against the draft. She told how she didn't want to be forced into the Army because, when growing up, her big brothers used to have fun tying her up, and she just wasn't physically strong enough to tie them up.

The next day, we had another rule thrown. Things got progressively tenser and uglier at the state capitol. On June 25, ERA supporters went to the local slaughterhouse, bought plastic bags of pigs' blood, and came back and wrote on our capitol's marble floors the names of the legislators they hated the most. Legislators found these tactics not persuasive, and Illinois voted down ERA one final time. On June 30, 1982, fifteen hundred battle-weary-but-triumphant Stop ERA volunteers gathered again in the ballroom of the Shoreham Hotel in Washington, DC, to savor our victory that the Equal Rights Amendment would die at midnight. A giant rainbow made of balloons rose high over the dais, and many political prestiges from President Reagan on down paid tribute. The heroes of the day were the women who came from the fifteen states that never ratified ERA, plus the five states that bravely rescinded their previous ratifications.

In the middle of the program, the hotel security guard rushed up to MC Bob Dornan to report that the hotel had received a phone call that a bomb had been placed in the ballroom. I made the decision to ignore the threat and not evacuate because, anticipating that a bomb threat would be the feminists' last tacky insult, I had arranged for the police dogs to sniff out the room beforehand and secure it.

Voice: *Phyllis*: *We have the people with the strength of character, and this battle we have waged has proved it. Thank you for being here.*

The evening closed with Bill and Prudence Fields singing the appropriate themes for our gala celebration: "The Impossible Dream" and "Great Day." And our most-favorite Eagle Forum singers, the talented and wonderful Christian couple Bill and Prudence Fields, are now going to give us a repeat performance of those songs.

## 1998

## San Diego, California
## Is It Safe to Send Your Child to College?

I s it safe to send your child to college? I have certain credentials for addressing this subject; I have three degrees myself, two that I got in the 1940s and one that I received in the 1970s, and then I have six children for whom I have paid forty years of college, undergraduate and graduate, education. So my family has quite a lot of experience with colleges. In addition to that, I have lectured or debated on more than five hundred campuses over the last twenty years. Undoubtedly, that's more than any other conservative; of course, it's not more than Jessie Jackson or Maya Angelou or Angela Davis or Louis Farrakhan, but I surely have been in more debates than anybody liberal or conservative, because when the liberal comes to the college campuses he gets the whole platform. When I come, I generally only get half the platform because, of course, they have to hear the other side.

And I've debated all the feminists about abortion and feminism: Betty Friedan and Sarah Weddington, who was the lawyer in *Roe v. Wade*, and Bella Abzug and Gloria Allred and Catharine MacKinnon, all the presidents of the National Organization for Women, Patricia Ireland, Eleanor Smeal, Karen DeCrow, Wilma Scott Heide, the head of Planned Parenthood, the head of the ACLU, politicians like George McGovern and dozens of female politicians.

Tonight I'm going to tell you the awful truth about college campuses, and, of course, there are a few campuses (not very many in this country, mostly religious) to whom these criticisms do not apply, but you'll have to look hard to find any of those. These are generalities that I'll put out, but as I say, they are based on visiting hundreds of campuses.

I believe that campuses should be subject to the "truth in labeling" requirements; they should carry warning labels to advise teenagers what they're getting into. It takes extraordinary smarts, detective work and maturity to select colleges and courses that give value for the price you are paying, now up to thirty-five thousand dollars per year at the elite universities. At most colleges, selecting courses is like eating at a cafeteria, where you have to choose the items by label only without ever seeing what is in the dish, where you cannot return it if it isn't what the label advertises, and where you cannot sue the management if you get food poisoning. It now takes most college students at least five years, and many six years, to get their BA or BS degree rather than the traditional four years. Unless you are unusually skillful in choosing your college and your courses, you will be conned, cajoled, or counseled into spending twenty-five or fifty percent more time and money for your diploma than you planned, but it will not be worth one penny more than if you graduated in four years. State universities are the worst at this, but when I spoke at Bowdoin, a fancy college in Maine, they bragged that ninety percent of their students graduate in five years. Now there's no valid reason for taking so long for college; the reason most often given is that students could not get admitted to the courses they need for their major or to graduate because there are not enough sections of the necessary and important courses that are given, so the students have to waste their college dollars taking trivial or worthless courses that do not advance them toward their degree.

Another reason is that the counselors urge students to take only three courses a semester instead of five, which drags out the college experience. Most university course catalogs are dishonest advertising because up to half of the courses listed are not really offered, or maybe offered only once in ten years. One researcher found that, at Harvard, of the forty-four courses in American history listed in the catalog, only ten were offered at any one time.

At the large universities, most undergraduate courses are not taught by professors at all, but by graduate students called "TAs," or "teaching assistants" who know very little more than the students they're supposed to be teaching. Harvard has eight hundred TAs posing as professors; Columbia has six hundred, and Princeton has five hundred. The average tenured professor teaches only six hours a week, and a third of them do not teach at all. Many tenured professors teach mostly seminars about extremely limited subjects that are worthless to the students. A lot of them are just rap sessions that require little or no preparation. Many important and necessary college courses, especially in math and sciences, are taught by instructors who can barely speak English. There is no excuse for a university hiring an instructor who cannot speak easy-to-understand English, and it is dishonest not to warn students about such instructors. I got my law degree at Washington University in the 1970s; I had one course from a student I could not understand because he was a foreigner with such poor English. I still feel cheated by that course.

Then there is the matter of grade inflation; don't think you're getting a good education just because you get good grades, because the grading practices are corrupt. At Stanford, ninety percent of the letter grades are As and Bs; at Princeton, eighty percent; at Harvard, A- stands for "average." Even SAT courses have been corrupted; the SAT management a couple of years ago added seventy points to all scores in order to disguise the fact that SAT scores have been dropping for twenty years.

Much of the college curriculum has been politicized by the liberals and the feminists; the radicals of the sixties are now tenured professors. The title of the course in the catalog may indicate a traditional course, but the assigned readings have frequently been changed. Instead of reading the great works of Western civilization—Aristotle, Shakespeare, Thomas Aquinas—many courses have censored out the "DWEMS," that's the "Dead White European Males," and they have shifted

112

to what we call oppression studies, that is, readings of third-rate feminists and minority writers who paint themselves as victims and attack Western civilization as sexist, racist, and oppressive. Many courses teach that Western culture and American society are inherently evil and that individual liberty itself is oppressive.

Now let's talk about political correctness, which is the prevailing environment on most college campuses in faculty bias, in course content, in visiting speakers, and in organizations and events that are funded by the student fees. Political correctness is the dogma on the campus. Let me give you a checklist of the particular tenets of political correctness: first, everything is political. All academic subjects must be seen through the prism of gender and race oppression, including history, literature, social relationships, and even private conversations. Second, victimology: every group is entitled to claim minority status as victims except, of course, white males and Christians. Third, multiculturalism: that's a code word for the false notion that Western civilization is bad and every other group, whether civilized or not, is superior. Multiculturalism is the only required course at all the sixteen state universities in New York State. Fourth, radical feminism:

the entire world must be seen as a big conspiracy against women, and all men are guilty, both individually and as a group. Joking about this doctrine is absolutely not permitted. The University of Wisconsin and the University of Connecticut both banned jokes; of course, we all know that the feminists have no sense of humor. Most prestigious colleges have more women's studies courses than they have economics courses; at University of California in Davis, the law review policy is to use the female pronoun as a matter of course except when referring to a criminal defendant, and then you use the male pronoun. At Arizona State University, the drama professor Jared Sakren was fired for producing Shakespeare's great play, "The Taming of the Shrew." Shakespeare is not "PC."

Affirmative action is the rule. Reverse discrimination in admissions, grading, and employment for groups that proclaim their status as victims is not only mandatory, it is non-debatable. Having sex with anybody anytime is okay, and may not be criticized. The social acceptance of homosexual behavior and activism is non-debatable. The code word for the gay rights agenda is "diversity," so look out whenever you see that word. And the seventh and final tenet of political correctness on this list is "tolerance." That is a code word meaning tolerance for politically correct views, but not for the politically incorrect. Tolerance means conformity to political correctness. Three hundred and eighty-three colleges have speech codes; Christianity is, of course, incorrect. In many colleges, students are not permitted to turn in papers that identify dates as B.C. (as in "before Christ") and A.D. (as in "*anno domini*"), and instead they must use "BCE" (as in "before the common era") and "CE" (as in "common era").

Now we have the matter of the dumbing-down of America's colleges. You think elementary and high schools have been dumbed-down? Well, so have the colleges. The National Association of Scholars, a prestigious group of college professors, published a devastating sixty-five page report on its investigation of the courses offered and required at the fifty top undergraduate colleges and universities, both public and private. This organization compared the college curriculum in the years 1939, 1964, and 1993. They concluded that universities have simply purged from the curriculum many of the required courses that formally taught students the historical, cultural, political and scientific basics of our society. The number of mandatory courses has been dramatically reduced from an average of 7 in 1939 to 2 1/2 in 1993. The former universal requirement that students take a basic survey course in several important areas has virtually vanished. Only 12 percent of universities now require a thesis or comprehensive examination to get a bachelor's degree; in 1964 more than half of them did. The college year has been shortened by about 1/4, leaving more time for spring break and other frivolities, but, of course, without any reduction in tuition price or professors' salaries. When I went to college, we had classes on 195 days per year; today's students have classes only 156 days per academic year. In 1964, 36 percent of universities had traditional mathematics requirements; now, only 12 percent do. In 1939 and 1964, more than 2/3 of universities required a basic science course; now it's only 1/3.

Now, meanwhile, the total number of courses offered on college campuses at undergraduate institutions has doubled; there are hundreds of courses, but that doesn't mean more opportunities to become an educated citizen. The majority of these additional courses are on narrow and idiosyncratic subjects of interest to the professors but almost worthless to the student. Now here are the titles of some of these thousands of courses that are taught at major universities that are really propaganda masquerading as education. At Pomona in the

English Department, you can take a course in "The Bear"—that is, "bear" as they have over at the zoo. In Columbia, in the English Department, you can take a course in "Sorcery and Magic." In Dartmouth, in the English Department, on "Queer Theory, Queer Texts." At Harvard, you can take a course on "Fetishism" and on "Feminist Biblical Interpretation." At Yale, there are courses in "AIDS and Society," and "Queer Histories." At Cornell, you can take a course in "Gay Fiction." At Princeton, you can take "Sexuality, Bodies, Desires and Modern Times." At the University of Pennsylvania, in the Religion Department, you can take "Feminist Critique of Christianity." At Brown—of course, that's where a lot of the children of our left-wing Presidents go—they can take a course in "Unnatural Acts: Introduction to Lesbian and Gay Literature." At Bucknell, they have a course in "Witchcraft and Politics." At Middlebury, in the Spanish Department, you can take "Female Erotic Literature of Latin America." At Stanford, in the History Department, you can take "Homosexuals, Heretics, Witches and Werewolves, and Deviants in Medieval Society." At Vassar, you can take "Global Feminism." At Williams, in the Anthropology Department, you can take "Witchcraft, Sorcery, and Magic." At Rutgers, "Homo Erotic Literature." At the University of Colorado, "Queer Theory." At the University of Massachusetts, you can get credit for "Rock and Roll." At the University of Michigan, you can take "Crossing Erotic Boundaries." At the University of Minnesota, "Gay Men and Homophobia in American Culture." At the University of North Carolina, "Magic, Ritual, and Belief." And at the University of Wisconsin, "Goddesses and Feminine Powers."

Now, these courses are not education; they're just propaganda, entertainment, and behavior modification. And the reason why your tuition is so high is that you're paying these high-priced professors to teach these worthless courses. At Princeton, part of your $33,000 per year tuition will be paying the salary of Peter Singer, the new professor of bioethics. He is an advocate of abortion rights, animal rights, and euthanasia rights. He teaches that the only reason we value life is the pleasure it enjoys: if cows lead pleasurable lives, don't butcher them. If handicapped lives are not pleasurable, kill them. Now who decides what's pleasurable or not? Of course, enlightened people like himself. Now the result is that our best colleges and universities no longer turn out graduates who have even an elementary knowledge of our civilization and our heritage. They do not learn the basic facts of our country's history, political and economic systems, philosophic traditions, and literary and artistic legacies. And quite apart from the fraud of charging an exorbitant price for a devalued diploma is the fact that we are in danger of losing the national cohesion of a known and shared heritage, which has sustained and nourished our unique institutions of freedom within limited constitutional government.

In addition, there's the dumbing-down that's inherent in giving courses that are not college courses at all, but are simply designed to teach students what they didn't learn in high school. Sometimes these courses are called "remedial." Such courses were unheard of when I went to college; today, such non-college level courses are offered in 70 percent of the elite universities, and most of them give college credit. Nationwide, 30 percent of entering freshmen must take remedial courses. In California, it's 50 percent. This means the taxpayers are paying twice. Recently, the California state legislators tried to pass some legislation to send invoices back to the high schools that deceived their students by giving them As and Bs and graduating them without learning anything. One day, I was on the public platform with former AFT President Al Shanker, and he said that when he was going through school, his parents could lay down the law to him and say, "Al, get busy and do your lessons or you won't get into college!" He said, "No parent can say that to his child today. Everybody can get into some college somewhere in the United States." Colleges and universities should abolish their remedial courses and admit only students who are capable of doing college work. But they're not going to do that because of the easy flow of taxpayers' money, which makes it so profitable for colleges and universities to admit all the students they can and then send the bill to the taxpayers.

Now let's talk about the campus activities. There's lots of money for left-wing activities on college campuses. This comes from a tax on all students called a "student activity fee." It is a real racket. Sometimes they call it "voluntary," but the plain fact is you can't get your grades or your diploma unless you pay it. Every student must pay. And where does this money go? It goes into groups of student leftists and is used to promote left-wing causes, speakers, publications, and politics. The radical left-wing movement is largely financed on the college campuses of this country, and it is an enormous amount of money: hundreds of thousands of dollars a year on the big university college campuses. At the University of Wisconsin, the student fee is $165.75 per student, per semester. This adds up to $974,200 in one school year, and it will be controlled by a little group of leftists who've gotten access to this money and dole it out to left-wing causes. One of Eagle Forum's main projects has been to sponsor campus groups called Eagle Forum Collegians, and our Collegians have made it a big project to cut off this money. Our first big project was several years ago in the University of California at Berkeley; this is when one of my sons was getting his PhD out there and found out all the money that was going to these left-wing causes. So, he got together with some students and they filed their claim in the small-claims court. In about an hour, they won their case. It was an open and shut case: the students were taxed, and their money was taken to give to causes they didn't believe in. Well, the great University then went and hired the most high-priced, prestigious lawyers in San Francisco; they moved it from the small-claims court into the "real court," as they say, and it took fifteen years to get the decision. At the end of fifteen years, we finally won it in the California Supreme Court at a case called *Smith v. Regents at the University of California*; the court said the students may not be forced to support causes they strongly oppose, and the court listed fourteen political or ideological groups to which the money of the University of California had been going, including the National Organization for Women, the Campus Abortion Rights Action League, the Gay and Lesbian League, the Spartacus Youth League, and the Feminist Alliance and lots of others. In fact, when my Roger was at University of California, they even put up the money to send a whole delegation of feminists out to Chicago to march with Phil Donahue in the pro-ERA demonstration. And the students were taxed for that.

Well, our next big breakthrough in this cause came just a few months ago in 1998 when the Federal Appeals Court ruled that the University of Wisconsin cannot constitutionally force students to pay into funds that give to organizations they oppose. The court decision cited eighteen student organizations that had been funded by student fees, including the Lesbian, Gay, Bisexual Campus Center, which distributed sexually explicit materials; the Campus Women's Center, which lobbied for abortion rights; the UW Greens, which distributed campaign materials for the Green Party and Ralph Nader's Presidential candidacy and organized a march against the governor's budget; the Madison AIDS Support Network; the International Socialists Society, which advocated the overthrow of government and disrupted a church meeting; the

Ten Percent Society, which lobbied for same-sex marriages; the Progressive Student Network, which lobbied against the GOP Contract with America; the United States Student Association, which lobbies for a whole mix of left-wing causes; the Militant Students Union, and the students of the NOW. You can see that the radical movement in this country is financed on the college campuses by student activity funds paid by your children; that is the way the racket works. The court, in this case out at the University of Wisconsin, cited Thomas Jefferson, "To compel a man to furnish contributions of money for the propagation of opinions which he disbelieves is sinful and tyrannical."

Indeed it is!

And what we are looking for now is students in the other circuits; see, we've gotten good decisions now in two of the nine circuits, but we do have the funding and the support to go forward with cases in the other circuits, because when a court of appeals court hands down the decision, it's only good in the states that are in that circuit. So if you have friends, children, grandchildren, nieces and nephews who would like to participate in this in other parts of the country, please contact us; we think this is one of the most important projects we've ever undertaken.

Now I want to give you some of my experiences in going to these college campuses to lecture or debate; I am usually invited as the token conservative or the token pro-lifer after they've had a whole list. When I went to Youngstown Ohio State University, they gave me a list of their previous speakers, and, just mentioning the feminists previous speakers, they had already had lectures from Bella Abzug, Gloria Steinem, Jane Fonda, Pat Schroeder, Katherine Brady (who talks about incest), Shirley Chisholm, Ellen Goodman, Germaine Greer, Wilma Scott Heide, Shere Hite of *The Hite Report*, Kate Millett and Sarah Weddington. So, after all that, they felt they needed to have a token on the other side, so they invited me.

A couple years ago, I went to speak at Old Dominion State University at Virginia, not a particularly left-wing school; their previous female speakers were extreme feminists Susan Faludi, Molly Ivins, Patricia Schroeder, the sexologist Dr. Ruth, Faye Wattleton of Planned Parenthood, and a lesbian army colonel. Nevertheless, the feminist faculty protested the invitation to me. When I did a debate on pro-life at the University of Michigan, the students wanted to get a big auditorium and they asked the Women's Studies Department to sponsor this debate—it was a debate; it wasn't a lecture—they refused because they didn't think my views had any right to be heard on the campus of the University of Michigan. So the students had to go to another department that was not dominated by the feminists.

I've done hundreds of these debates on abortion and feminism on the college campuses—a lot of them against Sarah Weddington, who was the lawyer in *Roe v. Wade*, many times before hostile audiences. The prevailing view on most of the college campuses is the feminist view that the unborn baby has no rights whatsoever. I've encountered all kinds of adverse behavior, negative behavior; a lot of picketing. I've been at a lot of colleges where students were walking around carrying signs saying, "I am a second class citizen," or the many abortion signs that they carry. Their rudeness, their rowdiness is really not to be believed; a lot of it is incited by the bitter female faculty. In the late 1970s, it was really the worst; it is not quite as bad now as it used to be then. I went to one university where their method of protest was to all light up marijuana when I was introduced; another one where their method of protest was to all engage in loud belching during my speech. I've had several cases where they had the bomb threat; we had to evacuate the auditorium and try to find someplace else. I had one college where they circled the back of the hall carrying paper plates of whipped cream threatening to throw it (I'm sure it was dream whip); one where the girls thought it was really neat to take their pants down and show their behinds at me; another one where I was speaking in a cafeteria with windows behind me and all of a sudden they were laughing and I wasn't saying anything funny, and there were streakers riding back and forth—maybe you all don't know what streakers are—riding back and forth behind me.

When I spoke at Georgetown University, they had some women who sat at the front row and they had decked themselves out with heavy clanging ball and chain to symbolize the oppression of women in this country. When I spoke at the University of Illinois, it was a particularly hostile audience, and after I had been speaking a little bit one of the fellows came up and grabbed my arm and he said, "I see spray paint in the front row; let's get out of here," and we got out fast.

When I spoke at Hamilton College in beautiful upstate New York and I talked about how ridiculous it was to let the women in the University of VMI, where they shave their heads and call you "Brother Rat;" three women shaved their heads in protest at my coming.

Well, when I went to the University of Wisconsin, known as the most left-wing college in the country, the University was so apprehensive about my coming that they had an armed guard meet me at the plane when I arrived in Madison. He stayed with me the entire time; they checked me into a motel under an alias, and they had twenty-two security people on duty the night I spoke.

Why do I go? Well, it's varied; you know, it's funny; it was the worst in the late 1970s, and then in Ronald Reagan's second term, students began to get more polite and more willing to listen, but then, in the late 1980s, this wave of political correctness set in, and there's a very bitter, ugly edge to a lot of it. I have usually very large crowds when I go to a college campus—very frequently a thousand students—and in this crowd there are usually a very small number who came to cheer for me and a very small number who came to cheer for my opponent, and a big majority came because there wasn't a good basketball game that night. So it's an opportunity to give a pro-life message to people who have never heard it before, and I've had some very rewarding experiences of young women coming up to me afterward and telling how they were influenced by the presentation that I gave.

Another thing that I tell these college girls, particularly when I talk about feminism, is to tell about the case of Anne Taylor Fleming, whom you sometimes see as a commentator on *MacNeil Lehrer*, *Newshour*, and some other programs. I debated her on *CBS Morning News* in the 1970s—about 1975 or '76—on abortion, and she made fun of my pro-life views and just ridiculed me and said that if she were pregnant now, she would have an abortion. Well, twenty years makes a great difference in a woman's life, and this is what I tell these young women: a couple of years ago, she wrote a book called *Motherhood Deferred*. Now, she's still a feminist; she doesn't agree with anything I say, but it is a very bitter book. She says, "I am a woman of forty who put career ahead of motherhood, and now long for motherhood. I belong to the sisterhood of the infertile. I'm a loathsome, babyless, baby boomer, now completely consumed with the longing for a baby. I am tempted to roll down the window and shout, 'Hey hey, Gloria Germaine Kate! Tell us how it feels to have ended up without babies, without children, the flesh of your flesh. Was the ideology worth the empty womb?'" It's a cry that the young women ought to hear while they still have time to make their own choices about what they want to do with their lives. Now I have some pieces of advice to students; have we got any in the room who are about to go off to college? I'll give you some helpful advice because, I guess, in our world you have to go to college.

First of all, pick your courses carefully; since you are paying an enormous hourly rate for classes, don't waste your education dollar on trivial, non-academic courses. We call them "guts courses." Easy courses that you can pass only with your gut instinct. Don't waste your dollar on rap sessions on highly specialized subjects of no interest to anybody except the professor. Seek out courses that teach the true history and achievements of Western civilization and the United States rather than multiculturalism, which is a code word for downgrading America. And I hope that we on our Eagle Forum website—which is a wonderful website you ought to tie into, and our Collegians section—we will be putting up the syllabus of a lot of courses that are dangerous to students, that they ought to look out for, which they wouldn't learn about from the catalog.

Secondly, I urge you to take engineering math and science; you learn things that are true, not things that are false that you have to unlearn later.

Third, examine the syllabus of the courses before you sign up. Remember, a traditional title is no guarantee of what the course really covers because so much of the college curriculum has been politicized by the liberals and the feminists to get rid of the dead white European males who wrote the great books of Western civilization; they've been censored out and replaced with all of these third-rate feminists and minority writers who want to tell us how much they are victims and how oppressed they are. Often, you can tell if the course has been politicized—not always, but often—by the use of certain words in the title. So here's a good checklist of words that betray the bias of the course: sex, sexuality, gender, diversity, lesbian, gay, women, feminism, race, queer, AIDS, female power, perverse, homosexuality, patriarchy, race, ethnicity, transgender, fetish, erotic, female power, magic, sorcery, and New Age, and any of those words is a very good clue that the course is probably propaganda, not education, and there are hundreds of courses that have those words in the title.

Now, if you take economics, seek out the professors who teach the successful free market economics according to Adam Smith or Milton Freedman, and try to avoid professors who teach the failed economics of socialism.

Fifth, be aware that English is one of the most corrupt of all the college departments. The English departments are infected with the disease that is called "deconstructionism." That means there is no such thing as intrinsic merit in a work of literature, and what matters is not what the author said, but what you think about the book. And under deconstructionism, there's no such thing as a classic, so one book is just as good as another.

Sixth, avoid women's studies; there's no excuse for taking women's studies courses. They are just propaganda courses for radical feminists and often lesbian ideology and behavior. You know the big mama of the feminist movement is Simone de Beauvoir, who wrote that marriage is an obscene bourgeois institution. She is the doctrinaire for women's studies, and anybody going to college should avoid any of these courses.

Seventh, pick your professors very carefully; avoid courses taught by teaching assistants who are just graduate students and who don't know much more than you do. Make sure you don't get trapped in a course that's taught by an instructor who doesn't speak intelligible English. Avoid most of the female faculty; most of them are bitter and cannot deal with opposing views at all, and avoid instructors that are so bigoted that they demand that you do not refer to dates as in "Before Christ" and "*anno domini.*"

Eighth, and this is important: avoid taking advice from college counselors. They are working for the college; they are not working for you. They are looking out for the financial interests of the college, not yours. The counselors frequently channel students into a schedule that ends up requiring five or six years to get a bachelor's degree because it is profitable for the college to keep you on campus an extra year or two. If you are not mature enough on your own to investigate and devise a plan of study and to select the courses that achieve that goal, you have no business going to college at all.

Ninth, watch out for crime on campus. Most colleges conceal the crime on campus and they lie about it; they don't report the actual amount of crime that takes place on college campuses.

And ten, realize that you are in moral danger every day and night on college. You know, the big topic on college campuses is date rape. Of course, I ask the question, what is the girl doing in the boy's bedroom? What did she expect to have happened? Avoid the heavy drinking parties; a recent article in *US News and World Report* said that 42 percent of the students engage in binge drinking. The prevailing opinion on campus is an overwhelming approval of casual sex. Harvard just named two lesbians as the housemasters to direct the social life of its most prestigious dorm. A large percentage of the girls on campuses have had abortions; that is obvious from the hostility and bitterness I encounter in my debates. I had one guy stand up in one of my debates in Los Angeles and, during the question period, say, "Well Mrs. Schlafly, we have to have abortion so I can enjoy the pleasure and intimacy of sexual intercourse." And that is just their up-front position. I sent our youngest child, Anne, to Georgetown University, and in her first year, her roommate had an abortion, the girl in the next room had an abortion, and the girl down the hall had an illegitimate baby—in fact, she had one every year by a different guy. So this is what's going on. At Yale University, there are four students who have had the temerity to challenge the requirement that they live in a co-ed dorm because they say that offends their religious views about chastity and decency. It's a big lawsuit; I hope they win, but they're not likely to. That's the situation; Yale is no worse than any other college in that respect.

The student should prepare himself morally and psychologically for freshmen orientation, which may be a culture shock. You might be asked to role-play what it's like to be gay, or told that if you object to co-ed bathrooms, you need psychological counseling.

Twelfth, pick your companions carefully. Many will not have your morality; many will have a chip on their shoulder. We sent one of our sons to Princeton; he was put in a suite with twelve guys. By Christmas, ten of the twelve were on drugs. The only ones who were not were my son and the fellow from Taiwan. I've had any number of girls tell me they had a roommate who brought their boyfriend in and had sex in the room. If your roommate is doing that or is on drugs or engages in obnoxious behavior that interferes with your studying, absolutely demand a change. On the other hand, I'm sure you can find, if you look for them, some companions who share your values and belief. I strongly urge all of your children and grandchildren and friends who go to college to join a support group so they can have some kind of life with normal students who have good values. There are a number of these support groups; we have Eagle Forum Collegians; there are the College Republicans; there are number of different pro-life clubs; there are Students for America, there are a number of them. Some of them are called conservative clubs. Work or write for the conservative newspaper so you can associate with normal people and not feel so absolutely alone.

Now I don't mean to discourage you about college; it is possible to go to college and, I mean, after all, all my children did survive, and they didn't get caught in any of these things, so yours can too, but you really have to work at it. You can get a good education almost anywhere, but you need to know where the battleground is, and you need to be forewarned and forearmed.

Now I have a little bit of advice to parents: first of all, I would urge you to have your college children live at home if it is at all possible. It's not only cheaper, but you're safeguarding your child from an immoral environment. I know that's not always possible, but I would say that would be number one.

Secondly, I would lay down the law that you're not going to pay or help pay for more than four years, and you'll give them a bonus if they get out in three years. Four years is long enough for any student of traditional age to spend in college, and frankly, I think three years is a better length; it took me only three years to go through college, and two of my six children went through Princeton in three years. A college degree is not worth any more if it takes you six years than if it takes you three years, but the cost differential is absolutely enormous. Would you miss some of these wonderful college experiences? Yes, but you will be substantially reducing the occasions of sin.

The out-of-pocket tuition cost is only part of the cost. The more destructive part of all these years in college is that so many young people between the ages of eighteen and twenty-five waste so many of their prime productive hours and years cruising along as an undergraduate. It's an artificial and unnatural deferral of maturity and of taking responsibility for your own life. I worked a forty-eight hour-a-week job the whole time I went to college, and while I was carrying a full college schedule, and it is very difficult for me to understand what they are doing with all that time.

Next, I would urge parents to put in an 800 phone number in your phone so that your child can call home free anytime from anyplace—dorm, restaurant, emergency, car wreck, or anything else—without trying to find a credit card or number or something else; it's very simple, you only pay on the 800 number when the call comes in. And very important, I urge you to get a computer so you can communicate with your college child on email; this is very important. We used to write letters; nobody writes letters anymore. They won't write you letters, but if you have an email, it's so easy to hit the "reply" point on the computer, and you can communicate with quick little messages every night. I have one son on each coast, and the last thing I do every night before I go to bed is to check my email and send just a little message to each one of them. That is the one way you can stay in touch with your children when they go off to college and won't write you letters and may not even call you up.

There are a number of wonderful books about what's going on in colleges; Tom Sowell has one called *Inside American Education*; Martin Anderson has one called *Imposters in the Temple*; George Roche has one on *The Fall of the Ivory Tower*, and Charles Sykes has one called *Prof Scam*. I recommend them all; you need to know what's out there before you embark on the college experience.

As Abraham Lincoln said, "The philosophy of the classroom today will be the philosophy of the government tomorrow." Look out, it's out there.

Good luck, and God bless.

# 1965

## Southern California

## What Are the Gravediggers Doing Now?

Madam President, distinguished guests, and good friends; I'm so glad that we started this evening with such a fine invocation. We should do all the praying we can before the Supreme Court declares any more prayers unconstitutional. Recently, my 8-year-old son had one of his friends over to dinner, and his friend looked a little lost when we said grace before meals. And so I said, "Steve, don't they say prayers before meals in your house?" And Steve replied, "No, my mother's a good cook."

I started my oldest child in a school where he would be taught Bible history at an early age, and one day I asked him to tell me something that he had learned. Well he said, "Mother, we learned about the Israelites and how they were captured by the Egyptians and put to work in the uranium mines. And then their leader Moses got a hold of some jeeps and they headed

139

for the Promised Land. And the Egyptians chased them with tanks and mechanized infantry, and just as they were about to catch them, they got to the Red Sea, and Moses put up a pontoon bridge and they escaped." And I said, "Johnny, I don't believe it really happened that way." Well, he said, "Mother, if you don't believe it happened that way, you sure wouldn't believe it the way the teacher told."

I'm glad you got that story; I told that story before one of my husband's groups of friends one night, and I don't think they knew what happened when Moses got to the Red Sea.

The question frequently asked in the last few months is the question: why did we lose so badly in 1964? Why—after we worked our hearts out, after we did more and better precinct work than ever before, after we had more money to spend than we ever had in a previous campaign—why did we still lose so badly? All events indicate that the decisive issue of the 1964 campaign was the issue of nuclear war. The majority of our people did not vote for Lyndon Johnson because he is photogenic. They voted for him because they were convinced by campaign oratory and television spots that he would better keep the peace than Barry Goldwater. *Newsweek* magazine said that ninety-seven percent of the Republicans who crossed over to vote for Lyndon Johnson did this on the issue of nuclear war. Also, we have seen reports that more than half of Johnson's votes from all sources came to him on this issue of nuclear war.

Now, the core of the issue of nuclear war in the 1964 campaign was this charge which was made by Barry Goldwater: under our present defense leadership, with its utter disregard for new weapons, our deliverable nuclear capacity may be cut down by ninety percent in the next decade. Senator Goldwater was referring to the drastic cutback in American bombers made by the policies of Secretary McNamara. When Goldwater made this charge, the Pentagon reacted quickly and vigorously. The Pentagon issued a statement saying that Goldwater's charge was false, misleading, and wrong, and then followed up with a great many statistics which got the issue so hopelessly confused that the American people didn't realize what the true facts were.

Secretary McNamara made political speeches and wrote articles in leading magazines such as the *Saturday Evening Post*, in which he repeated this confident theme. "A comparison of our nuclear forces with Russia's makes our superiority incontestable. In qualitative terms, it far exceeds three or four to one. There is no indication that the Russians are catching up or planning to catch up with the United States in strategic nuclear forces." Now, when you teach your children that Washington never told a lie, be sure to teach them that it was George, and not the city.

This is the Pentagon lie that won the election for the present administration. This is the core of the issue we face. McNamara and the administration claim we are three or four times stronger than the Soviets. Goldwater said they are reducing our strength by ninety percent. If enough of the American people had believed Goldwater before the election, surely a third of those who voted for Johnson would have switched, and the election would have gone the other way. Surely that many would have switched had they really believed that American military strength was in the process of being cut by ninety percent. But the issues became confused, and it was only after the election that the truth came out.

In March of this year, the Chief of the United States Air Force testified before a congressional committee that American bombers carry eighty percent of our deliverable nuclear capacity. Now, the difference between the eighty percent figure that he used and the ninety percent figure that Barry Goldwater used is more than accounted for by the 420 bombers that McNamara had scrapped between those two days. And when we examine the figures that are made available through congressional committees and through the Pentagon's own figures, we can establish the fact that McNamara has already scrapped seventy percent of our strategic bombers, and he has cut the bomb loads of our remaining bombers by sixty percent. This is what has happened under the policies of Secretary McNamara, and he has not built any new bombers, he has not replaced the ones which are worn out or destroyed in Vietnam. And soon we see that when Goldwater made the charge that the strength of the United States is being cut by ninety percent, he was not only correct, but he was, to use the appropriate term, "conservative" in his estimate. *US News and World Report* recently reported that our deliverable nuclear capacity is being cut within the next few years from 30,000 megatons to 2,000 megatons—a cut of well over ninety percent.

Now it is extremely important that we carry these facts to the voters so that they understand this issue of nuclear war which was the decisive issue in the 1964 election. I've been working for so long and and so hard in this educational field that sometimes I get weary, and I think I'm so old in the game that I can't quite remember whether it was Elizabeth Taylor or Will Rogers who said, "I never met a man I didn't like."

But don't be discouraged; we have to persist in this issue of defense because it is a matter of life and death to every American family. Let us look at the other areas of our strategic nuclear defense, besides the area of the bombers. First of all, there is the field of the super-megaton weapons. We know that McNamara is relying on the Minuteman missile, which is one megaton in strength. We know that the Soviets are building bombs of 50-100 megatons in size. How do we know they are building these bombs? Well, one way we know is because of the way that they violated and broke the nuclear test ban of several years ago. You don't have to take my word for it; just take the words of the United States Joint Chiefs of Staff who testified in 1963 that the Soviet Union was then ahead of the United States in the high-yield technology. That means in the super-megaton weapons. And absolutely nothing has happened since that time to change that estimate, except that we know the Soviets are racing ahead.

I think one of the best ways to describe the difference between the size of our bombs and the size of their bombs is to remember the story about the restaurant in Berlin during WWII that advertised "rabbit horse stew." The restaurant said that its stew was made with half rabbit and half horse. It just didn't tell its customers that it was made with one rabbit and one horse. And our bombs are to the Soviet bombs roughly as a rabbit is to a horse.

Let us look at the matter of bases. Several years ago, the United States had important, vital bases in Turkey, in Italy, and in other points close to the Soviet Union. And they had none close to us. Today, the situation is dramatically reversed. We have abandoned our missile and bomber bases in Turkey, in Italy, in Europe, in North Africa, and the Soviets have their base in Cuba, only 90 miles off our shore. Another area of the cutback in our military defense under Secretary McNamara is the scrapping of the important weapons on which the United States has spent millions or billions of dollars to develop. Great weapons, like the Skybolt and the Pluto and the B-7, on which your money has been spent for many years; but when these weapons were brought to the point where they were ready to go into production, they were canceled by Secretary McNamara.

Also, in the field of research and development, there has been striking and significant cutback. It takes more than five years to bring a new weapon from the drawing board to the firing line. We are not doing the development on such important weapons of the future as the orbital bomb, the neutron bomb, the gigaton bomb, the chemical and biological warfare weapons, and all of these we know the Soviets are racing ahead on. Now is it too late for us to do anything about it? Oh, no. America has all the resources to do anything we need to compete in the arms race. But this matter of being too late reminds me of the time I asked my long suffering husband the question, "Honey, don't you think married men are smarter than single men?" and to which he replied, "Yes, but by then it's too late." Well, it isn't too late, but it is mighty late. And just as falling bodies, the law of gravity tells us, pick up momentum as they fall, so these policies of Secretary McNamara are picking up momentum so that this dismantling of our military defense is proceeding at an alarming rate.

Now during these years, Secretary McNamara has said, "Well, yes, maybe I'm cutting back on the strategic weapons, but I'm concentrating on conventional weapons, so that we will have the conventional weapons we need to fight a limited war anywhere in the world." He called this a "flexible response." Vietnam gave us our first real chance to test what it meant, and Secretary McNamara's policy was found terribly wanting in Vietnam. In the spring and summer of this year, our men in Vietnam suffered shortages of almost everything that they needed to fight in Vietnam. They had shortages in transportation, in ordnance, in supplies, in ammunition, even in clothing. Our men were fighting in tennis shoes in a jungle where lack of the proper footgear could mean death because of the unusual weapons used by the enemy there.

And how is this possible, that we have these shortages? Well let me tell you one story which I know from personal experience. During WWII, I worked as a gunner and a technician in the largest ammunition plant in the world. We finished more than six billion rounds of ammunition. We had a peak employment of more than 42,000 people. At the end of WWII, the Truman Administration dismantled and scrapped the whole plant. They gave it away, sold some of it, and scrapped and destroyed the rest and turned the buildings into a record center. Then along came the Korean War, and the whole plant had to be reactivated. The machinery and the equipment had to be bought again, this time, of course, at a much higher

price, and the plant went into full production for the Korean
War.

At the end of that war, the Eisenhower Administration
did not make the same mistake that the Truman Administration
had made. The plant was not given away, but it was put in what
we call, "a layaway basis." All of the machinery was carefully
cleaned and breezed and covered. The entire plant was put in
perfect condition. Like this, it would have remained perfect for
twenty years, ready to produce ammunition on a day's notice.
The plant remained like this from 1955 until 1961, and then
came Secretary McNamara. In one of the gigantic giveaways of
all time, this entire plant was given to India, a special
appropriation was made for the task of crating all this
machinery and shipping it down to New Orleans, and then it
was sent over to India and it was installed on a site 155 miles
west of New Delhi. And there, this plant began producing
ammunition, just in time for the India-Pakistan War. And so we
have the situation that this great plant, which was twice paid
for by the American taxpayers, was in 1965 producing
ammunition to kill our friends in Pakistan, instead of to save
the lives of our own men in Vietnam. This is just one example
of the dismantling of our military strength under the policies of

Secretary McNamara and the present administration. If their policies were found so far wanting in a little war in Vietnam against a thirtieth great power, how can we rely on this administration to defend us against the Big Threat? And we know where the Big Threat is. We know that the men in the Kremlin have repeatedly promised to bury us and to dig our graves and to dump us in. Now it isn't the Russian people who want to bury us; they know how evil their masters are. Even behind the Iron Curtain they have a little humor, and the most popular joke behind the Iron Curtain today is this: What was the stupidest thing done in the Soviet Union this year? Answer: Being shot into space, circling the earth fifteen times, and then landing again in the Soviet Union.

But there are men in the Kremlin who are dedicated to world conquest, and they have worked their tricks on us many, many times. I think of their strategy against us really as a gigantic confidence game. The original confidence man was Stalin; he started life as a bank robber. And he pulled the wool over FDR's eyes so that, in 1943, just before Roosevelt left for Tehran, he said to one of his close associates, "I have just a hunch that all Stalin wants is security, and if I just give him everything I possibly can, and ask for nothing in return, *noblesse oblige*, Stalin will work for world democracy and peace." This was the great illusion of Tehran and Yalta, and Roosevelt went to those meetings, and Stalin fleeced him of control of Eastern Europe, China, and three votes in the UN.

Another one of these clever, smooth confidence men was Castro. He fooled all the liberals into thinking he was the Robin Hood of Cuba. We were told on the pages of the *New York Times* that Castro was the Abraham Lincoln of Cuba. Well now Castro is tall, and he's a lawyer, and he wears a beard. But no reasonable person could find any other resemblance to Abraham Lincoln. And yet this is what the liberals thought and told us, and after Castro had consolidated his power and sent all his enemies to the wall, he made a big speech, and he laughed at us. He said, "I've been a communist since my college days, but I hid it in order to deceive the people whose support I need."

Another one of these confidence men was Ben Bella of Algeria. His cause was espoused as far back as 1957 by a young senator named John F. Kennedy. And after Kennedy became president, he invited Ben Bella to come to Washington. And Ben Bella was the only man in history who received a twenty-one gun salute on the lawn of the White House. And the next day, Ben Bella went down to Havana and kissed Castro—and you would just have to be a communist to kiss Castro.

The prevailing view in Washington today is that the communists have used up their bag of tricks. They've turned over a new leaf, and now they've mellowed, and they're peace-loving, and they're going to get along in one happy world together with us. History, logic, and common sense tell us that this is just as foolish as the hunch that Roosevelt played in 1943. The plain facts are that the communists are getting ready to cheat us with the confidence game to end all confidence games. What is this new confidence game that they are working on us? The new one is that they are trying to convince us that we are in a period of détente. Now, détente is a five-dollar word which stands for "international togetherness." And they tell us that in this period of "international togetherness" we are all going to be such good friends that the Soviets will grow more like us and we will grow more like them, and we will have convergence, and we will live in one happy world together. The American people know this isn't true, but there are many men in Washington who, after they have dined enough on vodka and caviar, seem to be taken in by this confidence game. These men are men who have no faith in America, or its greatness, or the principles that made us a great land. These are men who have become convinced in their own minds that America cannot win the arms race, that the Soviets are bound to win. And therefore, the only way to avoid a nuclear holocaust is for us deliberately to dismantle our military strength so that the Soviets will feel secure and not attack. These are the men I call the "Gravediggers." They are not communists; they are card-carrying liberals. They are the ideological descendents of the men who were wrong about Stalin, wrong about Mao Tse-Tung, wrong about Castro, and wrong about Khrushchev sending his missiles into Cuba in 1962. These are men who have espoused this new, strange theory that it is safer to be weak than to be strong. And so these men have brought about a deliberate and a progressive dismantling of American military strength.

This policy was first outlined for the public by a man named Paul Nitze, who later became our Secretary of the Navy. He laid out this plan at one of the most important strategy conferences ever held. He espoused this theory that it is safer to be weak, and he called for the dismantling of American military strength. This was followed up by another very

extensive and similar, specific plan laid out by Roswell
Gilpatric in the important publication, *Foreign Affairs*. It was
espoused by such men as Walt W. Rostow and Jerome
Wiesner, who attended the Moscow Pugwash Conference in
December of 1960, and within a few weeks thereafter became
policymaking officials high in the Kennedy-Johnson
administration. Of course, Secretary McNamara is the principal
one who carries out the policies of these Gravediggers who
believe that we should make America second best in the arms
race. And every time Secretary McNamara would appear
before a congressional committee in order to announce that he
was scrapping or holding back on some new weapon, the man
he would call on to fortify his position was the Pentagon's
Chief of Research, a man named Harold Brown. And Harold
Brown would provide the intellectual gobbledy-gook to
confuse the congressmen so they didn't realize what
McNamara was doing. And now in the last few months, with
all this signifies, Harold Brown has been made our secretary of
the Air Force. The chief spokesman of the Gravediggers on
Capitol Hill is Senator Fulbright, who chimes in frequently
with such announcements that aid the enemy as telling the
Soviets they might as well go ahead and build the Berlin Wall

and his announcing that we should make major concessions in Vietnam.

One of their principal spokesmen in the press is Walter Lippmann, who is the one who gave the idea to Khrushchev in 1962 that he could demand our withdrawal from Turkey in exchange for his taking missiles out of Cuba. The principal theoretician of the Gravediggers is a man named George Kennan. He made an important speech just this year in which he clearly laid out to this important audience that we must place our hope for future peace on the humanity of the communists and the hope that they will not attack. In other words, we have no hope from American military strength; we have no hope from MC's minutemen. Our only hope is in the humanity of the communists, that they will not go ahead and inflict us with a nuclear holocaust. Most Americans believe that our best hope is in American military superiority. And yet these Gravediggers go right ahead with their plans dismantling our strength and circulating in top echelons in government their treatises in which they tell each other of their secret plans.

Another one of these men is William Foster, who is the head of the U.S. Arms Control and Disarmament Agency. This is the agency that has paid your money in order to finance many of these gravedigger treatises. One of them, for example, was the one called "Study FAIR." Don't be misled by the name: there's nothing fair about it. It is really a blueprint for national suicide. "FAIR" is an acronym which stands for "Focus on Arms Information and Reassurance." Believe me, it isn't reassuring, but it does give a lot of information about what's going on in the minds of the Gravediggers. This treatise says that we should beware of information about the enemy which is too informative. It says it is destabilizing to world affairs if we know too much about what the enemy is planning. It's much more stabilizing if we have inaccurate information about what the enemy is planning.

Study FAIR says that if we have a crisis, we should turn off our sources of intelligence, such as the U-2 planes, so that we won't become nervous about what the enemy is doing during the crisis. We should give the Soviets the right to veto the intelligence information that is passed to the President of the United States. If the Soviets get jittery anyway, we should give them the right to order our Polaris submarines to surface and to reveal their positions. Now how crap-coddy can you get? Back in ancient times, the Roman emperors used to call in certain soothsayers, and these soothsayers would open up the insides of a chicken, and they would look at the entrails, and then they would advise the emperors what to do. But this method of policy planning was sane and logical compared to having our defense policy dictated by Study FAIR and these other gravedigger treatises.

These are very grim subjects, very grim to all Americans because they concern your lives and the lives of your loved ones. But even in the midst of this grim subject, I think it's important that we keep our sense of humor, and I always liked to have a little fun with my politics. Earlier this year, I had the pleasure of seeing the famous Gilbert and Sullivan operetta, "H.M.S Pinafore." I'm sure you know the famous lyrics about the man who polished up the handle so carefully, and stayed at a desk and never went to sea, and now he is the ruler of the Queen's Navy. As I listened to this famous operetta, it occurred to me that it is most appropriate to the men who run our defense policies today. The tragic thing is that the men who are running our defense policy today are men without military experience, who have been brought in by the scientific, technological elite—by the Gravediggers—and they are the ones who are dictating the defense policy which is bringing about the unilateral dismantling of our military strength. And so I've written a little parody which I'm going to share with you this evening. With help from our pianist who will, I hope, drown out some of my false notes, the first stanza is dedicated to our Secretary of Defense, Robert Strange McNamara, whose chief qualification for the job was that he presided over probably the greatest business failure in all of history: the Edsel.

> When Mac was a lad he served a term as whiz kid in Ford's auto firm. He supported the left like ACLU, and promoted the Edsel, which wouldn't do. He promoted the Edsel, which wouldn't do. He promoted the Edsel that's failed and gone, so now he is the ruler of the Pentagon. He promoted the Edsel that's failed and gone, so now he is the ruler of the Pentagon.

Thank you. You encouraged me. There's more. The second stanza is dedicated to Roswell Leavitt Gilpatric. Gilpatric was for several years the number-two man in the Pentagon, second only to Secretary McNamara. He is now the chairman of a special committee, which has drafted a secret report to determine what our nuclear strategy will be, which the

American people have not been permitted to see. His chief qualification for the job was that he was a lawyer, and, as described by the *New York Times*, he belongs to the "cream of the cream of ballroom dancers."

> When Gilpatric was a lad, he served a term, as office boy to an attorney's firm. He acquired three wives and a partnership, but of military strategy he had no grip. Of military strategy he had no grip. Of military knowledge he lacked all pretense, so they made him Deputy Secretary of Defense. Of military knowledge he lacked all pretense, so they made him Deputy Secretary of Defense!

> The third stanza is dedicated to our new Secretary of the Air Force, Harold Brown.

> Since Harold was a lad, he's never flown an aeroplane or worked on his own. He stayed at a desk and avoided every war, and scrapped new weapons for boys fighting over thar. He scrapped new weapons for boys fighting over thar. He canceled the B-70 and big missiles, of course, so now he is the ruler of our Air Force. He

canceled the B-70 and big missiles, of course, so now he is the ruler of our Air Force!

And the last one is dedicated to our Secretary of the Navy, Paul Nitze, who was the first one to promote some of these ideas that it's safer to be weak.

When Nitze was a lad, he served a term as office boy to an investment firm. He said the Soviets meant us no harm, and told all the churches that we should disarm. He told all the churches that we should disarm. He took disarmament so constantly that now he is the ruler of our whole Navy. He took disarmament so constantly that now he is the ruler of our whole Navy!

Funny yes, but tragic, that these are the men who are dictating the defense policies of the United States. The question that immediately comes to mind is, well, maybe we do have some of these way-out Gravediggers who have these fantastic plans, but how could they persuade Lyndon Johnson to go along with their schemes? Lyndon Johnson enjoys enormous power and prestige as the President of the United States. He would have more to lose than anybody else if the Soviets committed their attack against us. Why would he go along with the Gravediggers' plans? Well, let's look at it this way. When Lyndon Johnson suddenly became President in November of 1963, he succeeded a popular young President who had a great deal of that magic thing they call "image." LBJ had been the "forgotten man" around Washington. He had never been really accepted by the Liberals. He was faced with the task of how was he going to make an impact on the voters? He knew he had only a few months before he had to face the next election, and he wanted a plan in order to make sure that he would be reelected. At this point, he apparently decided that the way for him to do that was to go all out for the Great Society. He decided to go all out for more gigantic spend-and-spend, elect-and-elect social welfare schemes than had ever been conceived by the New Deal, the Fair Deal, or the New Frontier. And by the time Johnson put Hubert Humphrey on the ticket with him as Vice President, he had come full circle to this point of view. There was only one problem: the Great Society would be very expensive. Where was the money to come from? If the money came from increased taxes, even the most trusting voters would see through the fraud. Lyndon Johnson had no scruples about deficit financing, but he was afraid of topping the magic figure of the $100 billion budget. He might have squeezed it out of some other parts of the budget, but this is difficult to do, even for a team that is dedicated to economy (which the liberals certainly are not).

Now, at this crucial point, the Gravediggers came into the picture. And the Gravediggers said to Johnson, "We can provide you with all the money you need. We can give you all the billions you need to finance all of your great society projects. We can give you the money that will make you go down in history as the greatest humanitarian of all time. And this will assure your election and reelection for as long as you want to run. We can give you $2 billion in your first fiscal year; we can give you $8 billion in your second fiscal year, and we can give you $12 billion in your third fiscal year and after that."

Where was the money to come from? It was to come from our strategic defense budget. And this is the exactly what has happened. Under the previous democrat administrations, there was always great taxpayer opposition to the spending programs of Roosevelt and Truman and Kennedy. Today, we don't see that organized opposition, and the reason is because it looks like Lyndon Johnson is a miracle man; he can finance all of the Great Society projects and at the same time reduce taxes. And so the American people don't think it's costing us anything. But the money is coming from our strategic defense budget. Newsweek magazine called this the "slicing of the defense melon;" Lyndon Johnson and his political friends have been slicing the melon skillfully in order to provide these vote-buying schemes to guarantee large blocks of voters. He said in one of his speeches in the East Room of the White House, "We are taking money from the tanks and bombs and are putting them into the Great Society projects." This is what has happened, and the proof of it is in the budget figures which show that the money spent for our strategic defense—the only defense that can save us from the danger we face—has been reduced 45 percent in the last three years. This is how it has happened, and this is what has brought our country to a situation of great peril.

The matter of our national defense is not something we can leave to the Pentagon. Each of us has a part in this job of preserving American defense today.

First, we must nourish and sustain our faith in God, faith in America, and faith in the ideals that made our land great.

Secondly, we must continue to do the educational work that all of you have been doing so hard for the last year. God told Abraham that the cities of Sodom and Gomorrah would be spared His wrath if only ten just men could be found. And when ten could not be found, fire and brimstone descended on those cities. Our cities can be spared the fires of a nuclear holocaust if we can find ten patriots in each community who will tell the defense story and demand that we have the American strength to save us.

Third, we must engage in the political action which is necessary to do the job. We must work our precincts with fidelity and devotion so that we know that the American people have the facts and the message. "Fire the Gravediggers" must become a slogan that every politician understands.

Last Christmas Eve, I was doing my last-minute shopping, and I found myself late in the afternoon on a crowded elevator with many women with aching feet and arms full of bundles. Suddenly, the elevator gave a jerk, and one woman called out to the elevator operator, "Miss, if the cable breaks, will we go up or down?" The elevator operator had had her share of strain that day, too, and she turned around and calmly replied, "Madam, that will all depend on what kind of life you've been living."

And finally, the quality that we must have in this fight is old-fashioned bravery. We wonder whether we have enough Americans with the bravery to take on the task of the nuclear space age. But I am encouraged by the massive demonstration of bravery we had in 1964. Barry Goldwater was smeared with the most terrible campaign of terror that we have ever seen in American politics. Lyndon Johnson clearly implied in his campaign speeches that if Barry Goldwater were elected, it might result in one hundred million American deaths. Little girls eating ice cream cones on television appeared about to be incinerated in the nuclear holocaust if the voters voted against the administration. And yet, in spite of this campaign of nuclear terror, twenty-seven million Americans looked that terror in the face and went out and worked their hearts out for the candidate they felt could save the country. These twenty-seven million must again display this same kind of bravery in the nuclear space age. On this issue of defense, they can enlist with the many more millions to get the job done. Nuclear power can be the greatest power for good in the history of the world, providing America has the superiority. And it is up to us to demand and insist that we do have the strength, sufficient strength to make it ridiculous for any aggressor to attack.

The moment of truth for every American is when he looks into his heart and faces the evidence and resolves to go out and win the battle of the grassroots versus the Gravediggers.

## February 13, 1962
## Illinois
## The Relation Between Communists, Socialists and
## So-Called Liberals

I would like to compliment the Madison County Medical association in its civic-mindedness in putting on this forum. As one who has tried to put on quite a few meetings, I know that nice, large meetings like this one tonight don't just happen. They are the result of careful planning and hard work and you should be grateful to the doctors who have arranged this meeting for you.

The Fulbright Memorandum is something which you are all acquainted with. In the Fulbright Memorandum, it tells about the anti-communist seminars in which our military leaders participated. And in describing these anti-communist seminars, the Fulbright Memorandum says this: "The thesis of the nature of the communist threat often is developed by

166

equating social legislation with socialism and the latter with communism. Much of the administration's domestic legislative problems, including the continuation of the graduated income tax, expansion of social security (particularly medical care under social security), federal aid to education, etc., under this philosophy would be characterized as steps toward communism." Now this statement from the Fulbright Memorandum is exceedingly interesting, not only because it explains the motives for the muddling of the military and the statements against anti-communists by certain prominent politicians, but also because it constitutes an admission by a liberal such as Senator Fulbright that there is a provable equation between communism, socialism, and the so-called liberalism. And I would like to attempt to qualify some of these "isms" for you this evening.

Many people are still under the illusion that communism is an ideology, a philosophy, a form of government, a political party, or an economic system with which we can engage in polite parlor debate or in friendly competition and coexistence. The first essential to our understanding of communism is to realize that communism is a conspiracy of criminals who are waging war on the whole fabric of Western civilization. Communism is an international criminal conspiracy based on atheism, materialism, and economic determinism, organized on totalitarian lies with the power in the party, and dedicated to using all illegal and immoral means toward achievement of its goal of world conquest. Communists are not moral humans who operate as reasonable or rational human beings. Their so-called philosophy is so illogical that its fallacies could be exposed by the average high school student. Its economic system is a total failure and has brought nothing but poverty and famine. This was illustrated by the joke they tell about the Russian schoolteacher who asked his class one day, "Who were the first man and woman?" And one child replied, "Adam and Eve." And the teacher said, "What nationality were Adam and Eve?" And the child replied, "Why, Russian of course." And the teacher said, "How do you know?" And the child answered, "Well, it's easy. They had no clothes to wear, they had no roof over their head, they only had one apple between them and they called it Paradise."

We must realize that communists are criminals who use words and ideas as weapons to deceive us. When they say they want peace, they mean they want to conquer the world one "piece" at a time. When they invite us to peaceful coexistence, they mean we should "coexist" as the man on the gallows "coexists" with the rope around his neck. When they ask us to have a "sane" nuclear policy, they mean we should be "sane" like the prisoner at Alcatraz who realizes it is futile to try to escape. The communists are masters of deceit whose sport is to guile us into trusting them so that they can enjoy the fun of killing us.

The best indication of what goes on in the communist mind is revealed by a conversation that American Ambassador William C. Bullitt had with General Boris Shilov (a high official of the communist party)—a conversation which took place in the Kremlin. General Boris Shilov said, "I think the most extraordinary thing we did was to capture Kiev without fighting." And Ambassador Bullitt said, "How did that happen?" General Boris Shilov said, "Well, there were 11,000 czarist officers and their wives and children in Kiev, and they had more troops than we had, and we never could have captured the city by fighting, so we used propaganda and we told them that they would be released and they would be allowed to go to their homes with their families and would be treated as well as possible by our army. They believed that and surrendered." And Ambassador Bullitt said, "What did you do then?" And General Boris Shilov said, "Oh, we shot the men and boys and we put all the women and girls in brothels for the army." And Ambassador Bullitt said, "Do you think that was a very decent thing to do?" And Boris Shilov replied, "My army needed women, and I was concerned with my army's health and not with the health of those women, and it didn't make any difference anyhow because all the women were dead within three months."

Now that is the mentality and the morality—the immorality—of the communists who are entertained almost daily at the White House by the State Department and in the United Nations. The communists followed the strategy which was laid down by Dmitry Manuilsky in 1931 at the Lenin School of Political Warfare when he said, "War to the hilt between communism and capitalism is inevitable. Today, of course, we are not strong enough to attack. Our time will come in 20 or 30 years"—that's right now, of course.—"To win we shall need the element of surprise; the bourgeoisie will have to be put to sleep. We shall begin by launching the most spectacular peace overtures on record. The capitalist countries, stupid and decadent, will rejoice to cooperate in their own destruction. They will leap at another chance to be friends. As soon as their guard is down, we shall smash them with our clenched fists." That is the strategy that the communists have been following to capture the United States. Now what relation has socialism to this criminal conspiracy called communism? Many people have been led to believe that socialism is a respectable political doctrine. We hear people say that democratic socialism is something which is perhaps a fine thing, something which we should encourage other countries, particularly Latin America, to try to achieve. First, we must realize that communists use the words "socialism" and "communism" interchangeably, and as synonyms. All the communist writers from Marx and Engels through Lenin and Stalin, Khrushchev and Mao Tse-Tung to the present writers for communist publications use the words "communism" and "socialism" interchangeably. The word, the initials USSR, stand for "Union of Soviet Socialist Republics." The top communist publication in this country, *Political Affairs*, is subtitled, "A Theoretical and Political Magazine of Scientific Socialism." Now we must know also that communists used the term "socialism" to describe a transition stage on the way to communism. And this is really well illustrated by the words of John Strachey, who is a top English communist, in his book

*The Theory and Practice of Socialism.* Mr. Strachey said this, and I quote, "It is impossible to establish communism as the immediate successor of capitalism. It is accordingly proposed to establish socialism as something we can put in the place of our present decaying capitalism. Hence, communism works with the establishment of socialism as a necessary transition stage on the road to communism." Therefore, it is fair to say that the communists look upon socialism, such as they have in India under Nehru and Krishna Menon and in British Guiana under Cheddi Jagan, as transition stages on the way to communism. The use of this strategy for the United States of America was made very clear in this book, this rather famous book, called *Toward Soviet America* written by William Z. Foster for generations of top communists in the United States. In this book, Mr. Foster says this: "From capitalism to communism through the intermediary stage of socialism; that is the way American society is headed." And for his service to the communist party over many years, William Z. Foster is today one of only three Americans who are buried inside the Kremlin.

Socialism is much harder to define than communism because it doesn't always mean the same thing. There are a number of different socialist parties that have been on the ballot in several of our states. Socialists may differ on some minor or particular issues. They do not always follow a hundred percent the dogmatic lines laid down by the central authority such as the Kremlin. Several years ago on radio on the famous town hall of the air debate, Clare Luce asked William Z. Foster, the author of this book and top communist, this question: "Mr. Foster, can you name one issue on which you have ever differed with Stalin?" And Foster couldn't name one. And Mrs. Luce prodded him and said, "Not even one?" And Foster said, no, he couldn't name one because Stalin was always right.

Well, now socialists don't always have that absolute blind obedience to the line laid down from above. But socialists do have three fundamental characteristics which we must recognize. First of all, they are Marxists. And Marxism (socialism) is another branch of the same evil creed that produced communism. The socialists are materialists, and they promote the class war just as the communists do. Secondly, the socialists believe in government control and regulation of almost every aspect of our daily lives. And thirdly, in the international field, socialists promote world government under international socialist control.

Now when you realize that these are the three fundamental premises of socialism, it is then easy to understand that it is a complete myth that socialism can ever be a defense against communism. That is one of the fallacies we are told: that building a socialist government is a defense against communists. Socialists can never be anti-communist. They can be anti-Russian. They can be anti-firing squad and anti-slave labor camps. They may be anti-Khrushchev and anti-Castro. But they cannot be anti-communist because, by the fact of believing in socialism, they have already accepted the fundamental premises of communism. The differences that the socialists have with the communists are really like quarrels over a roadmap by people all of whom are in a hurry to get to the same place. Now that is why the socialists joined with the communists in a united front against anti-communists: they are partly like people who belong to a family and they may quarrel bitterly among themselves, but they present a united front when anyone from the outside attacks them. And we can illustrate this by reference to the socialist party platform of 1960. I will read you a passage from it. "We urge a campaign to root the institutions of McCarthyism out of our life: Repeal of the

Smith Act, and pardon of all its victims; abolition of the
Attorney General's Subversive List; repeal of the Loyalty Oath
Provision of the National Defense Education Act; abolition of
the House on Un-American Activities Committee and the
Senate Internal Securities Subcommittee." I know that all of
you here will recognize those platform planks as features of the
current communist line.

There is another illusion about socialism: that is it
communism without the firing squad. But it is not true that
socialists do not believe in force. One of the most prominent
socialists in the world, Nehru, proved that just a few weeks ago
when he seized Goa. The fact is that socialists are quite willing
to use force anytime they think they can get away with it. Now
one of the most prominent socialists of all time was the
playwright George Bernard Shaw. And in his book, called *An
Intelligent Woman*'s *Guide to Socialism*, G.B. Shaw says this:
"I often made it quite clear that socialism means equality of
income or nothing, and that under socialism, you would not be
allowed to be poor. You would be forcibly fed, clothed, lodged,
taught, and employed whether you liked it or not. Now if you
discover you have not the character and industry to be worth all
this trouble, you might possibly be executed in a kindly

manner. But while you were committed to live, you would have to live well." Thus we can see that the key difference between communism and socialism is, as George Bernard Shaw stated, under socialism "you might be executed in a kindly manner."

Now on the other hand, it's not true that the communists always use force. And we have an illustration of how communism can come to a country without the use of any force at all, and that is by this new book, called *And Not a Shot is Fired*. This book was written by Jan Kozak, a top official of the Czechoslovakian Communist Party. And this is the secret report which he made in 1957 at the University of Prague, which was never intended to be known by the West. In this report, Jan Kozak tells how the communists plan to take over a democratic, representative form of government by simply legal means and without the use of weapons or force. He explains it in these words, and I will read to you from the book: "All the changes which in their entirety represent a revolutionary transformation of a capitalist society into a socialist one will proceed absolutely legally."

Czechoslovakia is the pattern that the communists are using for the takeover of the United States, and this book shows how Czechoslovakia was taken over by legal means without the firing of a shot. On January 16, 1961, Khrushchev added further evidence to this; he said, "The transition to socialism in countries with developed parliamentary traditions"—that would be such as America—"may be affected by utilizing the national legislature." In other words, the communist strategy against the country may proceed by the use of simply legal means, without the firing of a shot, so that we would be behind the Iron Curtain as Czechoslovakia is today.

We must also be on guard for those communists who were actually part of the criminal conspiracy or who adopt the exterior of socialism in order to deceive people or to work their way into places where they might not be welcome if their true red colors were known. Now for example, Cheddi Jagan of British Guiana is a communist. But on his recent trips to this country, he called himself merely a "socialist" and a "Marxist" in order to deceive a lot of gullible people into giving him handouts from the American taxpayers' money. All the evidence points to the evidence that fact that Castro, Ramanand, Gouzenko, Abdullah, Sukarno, Nkrumha, Tito,

Perez, Manon, and Betancourt are agents of the communist conspiracy; they have adopted the disguise of socialism in order to grab handouts from the American Treasury and to have the Americans taxpayers patch their economic system. For example, Betancourt of Venezuela, who is a terrific writer, stated this, and I quote: "Let me point out to you here, publicly and openly, that I have been called a communist. But I think we should act in a little more thoughtsy way in this time to win what we need." That is what they do, isn't it? They act in a "thoughtsy" way in order to deceive another into believing that they are not really communists.

This is a book which shows very clearly how communists can use the disguise of socialism in order to get into areas where they would not be welcome if their true red color were known. This book, which is in many libraries and colleges, is called *Toward a Socialist America;* it's disguised in a beautiful red, white and blue jacket. Now this book is a symposium, with different articles by different writers, and in each article it gives you a little paragraph telling you about the author. One article is by John Howard Lawson, and they tell you he is one of the country's leading playwrights. They do not tell you that John Howard Lawson was one of the Hollywood ten who served a prison term for refusing to testify about their communist activity. They have a chapter by Herbert Aptheker, whom they tell you is a noted journalist. They do not tell you that Herbert Aptheker is the editor of the number-one communist magazine, *Political Affairs*. They have a chapter by Paul M. Sweezy, whom they tell you is one of the country's leading educators at the University of New Hampshire. They do not tell you that Paul Sweezy was put on the witness stand and asked the question, "Did you advocate Marxism in your classes?" And Professor Sweezy refused to answer. They have a chapter by Victor Perlo, and they tell you he is an economist and consultant. That is the understatement of all time. They do not tell you that Victor Perlo was the head of one of the most notorious Soviet espionage cells that ever operated in this country. And they have a chapter by W.E.B. DuBois, whom they tell you is a great champion of peace. They do not tell you that W.E.B. DuBois holds the all-time record for belonging to communist fronts (he belonged to 104), and on November 26, 1961, at the age of 93, he finally joined the Communist Party.

Now this is just an example of how communists can worm their way into our schoolrooms, onto the shelves of our libraries, into the avenues where they would not be acceptable otherwise, but disguised as socialists. One part of the subject which is frequently overlooked in any discussions of socialism is National Socialism. Now most socialism is international, but there is one type of socialism which is called "National Socialism." The abbreviation for National Socialism is "Nazi." Now one of the greatest hoaxes that has ever been put over on the American people is the myth that communism and Nazism are at opposite ends of the political spectrum. The purpose of this hoax is quite clear: it is to make you think that Nazis are right-wingers and, therefore, somehow ideologically allied with conservatives, and in that way to discredit conservatism in America.

And then there is a second false proposition that closed the rift; and that is, that we mustn't be too anti-communist because Hitler was anti-communist, and look where that led the world. Now these two fallacies are taught in many of the universities of our country, and they have been accepted by many intelligent but unthinking Americans. The fact of the matter is that both of them are hoaxes; they are complete fabrications made out of whole cloth. Nazism is a branch of the same evil Marxist tree that produced communism and socialism. Communism, socialism, and Nazism are blood brothers; they are all socialists. And Nazis are left-wingers, not right-wingers: they believe in the totalitarian control of our daily lives through the instrument of the party. And they have nothing—none of them have anything—in common with the American constitutional republic and our free economic system. Furthermore, it is not true that Hitler was anti-communist; he was the most notorious pro-communist of all time. The communists helped Hitler to power, and, after Hitler was in power, he signed the famous—the infamous—Nazi-Soviet Pact of 1939 by which Hitler and Stalin divided up Europe. And when Hitler went to war with Stalin, it was not from any ideological difference, but was simply a case of two bandits "falling out" over the division of the loot. We come now to the fourth branch of this subject, which is made up of the Fabians, the Keynesians, and the so-called Liberals. The Fabians were the originators; their thinking was carried on by the Keynesians, and those who have now espoused that philosophy have disguised themselves as Liberals. Fabianism began in England in 1880. Now the Fabian society was a society made up of socialists, most of whom were wealthy and educated and who, therefore, had easy entrée into intellectual, government, academic, social and financial circles. But these socialists were realistic; they knew that the English-speaking

181

people would never fall for an uncouth, revolutionary, shouting subversion on a soapbox. And so what the Fabians did was to give socialism a shave and a haircut. Respectability. And they adopted tactics of patience, of gradualism, and of penetration of existing institutions. Where the extremists were not welcome, the Fabians were welcomed because they had the "velvet glove" approach. The Fabians understood, as the socialists and communists did not, that it is much easier to subvert the sons and daughters and wives of the prominent and well-to-do than it is to impress the laboring classes. So this very clever artisan of disguising their real purposes has had phenomenal success.

It was not so long before Fabianism was introduced into America. It was brought to Harvard University and, from there, spread to the rest of the academic community. And the British Fabian leaders came over here in order to train Fabian leaders in America and just thought up the Fabian society in this country, which was known as the Intercollegiate Socialist Society. Some of the prominent people who were members of the Intercollegiate Socialist Society in their youth include Walter Lippmann, Louis Boudin, W.E.B. DuBois, Roger Baldwin and Stuart Chase.

Now by 1919, the Fabians had adopted the theories of a man by the name of John Maynard Keynes as their official policy. Now this man names Keynes was a socialist—a British socialist—and an atheist who believed that the government should control nearly every aspect of our daily lives. He did not even believe in private enterprise in the family, but felt that government should control the birth rate and break up the family as a free and independent unit. Mr. Keynes wrote a number of books, of which the best known is one called *The General Theory.* Now the average American citizen will find Keynes' book a mass of confusing verbiage. But, in spite of this, his works have had enormous influence. To put it in a nutshell, the Keynes Theory is this: First, that the government should control and regulate every aspect of our lives. And secondly, that extravagance is a great virtue, and thrift and saving are great vices.

Now you may think that sounds ridiculous, and of course it does. But the plain fact is that this theory has had enormous influence and that it is the prevailing theory accepted today in government and academic circles. We have to realize that there were some Fabians or Keynesians who were actually members of the communist conspiracy but who used Fabianism or Keynesianism as a cover for their Soviet activity. The best example of this is Harry Dexter White, who was dubbed as America's "chief Keynesian economist" by no other person than John Maynard Keynes himself. Keynes and White were close personal friends. Now Harry Dexter White was a Harvard professor—economics professor—who parlayed his prestige at Harvard into a job with the Treasury Department and rose to be the number-two man in the Treasury Department and the chief financial policymaker of the United States. He was the chairman of the Bretton Woods Conference. He set up the International Monetary Fund. He was the author of the Morgenthau Plan. He was the chief organ of the Keynesian manipulations in the United States. It was White who was the one who gave the printing rights to Soviet Russia for printing money—occupation money—which had to be redeemed by the American taxpayers. Now, White was finally exposed as a Fabian espionage agent, and then it was clear to many people that he had used his Keynesianism as a cover for his subrogate Soviet activity.

Another Harvard economics professor who was a Keynesian was Lauchlin Currie, and he also rose from that job to join the government and ultimately rose to be an administrative assistant in the White House itself. Likewise, Lauchlin Currie used Keynesianism as a cover for his underground activities for the Soviet Union. After Currie was exposed, he fled to South America out of reach of U.S. subpoena, and he is now serving as an advisor to the Columbian Government in order to help the Columbian Government decide how to spend the American foreign aid that we're going to give Columbia under the Alliance for Progress Code.

In addition to those Keynesians who were actual members of the Communist Party, there were others who were not members of the communist conspiracy but who willingly permitted themselves to be used as transmissions remotes for the spread of communist propaganda. Now a good example of this is a couple known as Sidney and Beatrice Webb. Now the Webbs were the leaders of the Fabian movement for more than forty years, and they were pawned off on an unsuspecting world as the astute thinkers, brilliant writers, and reasonable and respectable people. Well, in 1952, a man by the name of Igor Bogolepov testified under oath before one of our government committees. Mr. Bogolepov had been an official of the Soviet Foreign Office, and he testified that in 1945 Sidney and Beatrice Webb had made a trip to the Soviet Union where they had been given two books, which were written by Bogolepov and other members of the Soviet Foreign Office. And the Webbs went back to England and published these two books as their own work. That shows how they were willing to allow themselves to be used to spread Soviet propaganda under their name, all the while that all the people thought that the Webbs were a fine, patriotic English couple.

Now, the terms of "Fabians" and "Keynesians" are now passé. They're out of date; you don't hear people say that they're Fabians or Keynesians anymore. But the theories which they produced are the prevailing theories in government and in education today. The elder statesmen of Keynesianism in this country, Professors Alvin Hansen and Seymour Harris of Harvard, were proud to be known as Keynesians; they were there when I was there. They're proud to be called Keynesians. But the younger crop of intellectuals who follow in their same general theory and who are Keynesians at heart, such as Arthur Schlesinger, Jr., and J. Kenneth Galbraith, also Harvard professors, prefer to call themselves liberals. And the Keynesians have trained a whole generation of these liberals,

186

especially in the field of economics. Their chief organization is the Americans for Democratic Action, which has grown in power and influence so that there are now forty members of the Americans for Democratic Action who hold high-ranking, policymaking jobs in the federal government. Now the fundamental theory of these liberals is that the American people have too much money, and the government has too little money, and the people don't know how to spend their money wisely, so we should have more taxes in order to allow these liberals, through the government, to spend our money for us. Well, they say that if Patrick Henry thought taxation without representation was bad, he should see taxation *with* representation! But it's a pretty good rule of thumb that whatever the issue, these liberals are always going to line up on the side of spending more money or giving more power to the federal government.

Now most of the liberals are sincere, patriotic Americans—I have many friends who are liberals, and they're some of the most attractive people I know, but they don't consider themselves even socialists; they're fine Americans. But the liberals, nationally speaking, have found it impossible to provide the leadership and the action we need in order to fight communism because they have accepted the fundamental premises of socialism. You can prove this to yourself by taking the *Communist Manifesto*, laid down in 1848 by Marx and Engels, and seeing how many of the "Ten Points" the liberals are in agreement with today, such as the heavy progressive income tax. Now take, for example, Arthur Schlesinger, Jr., who was surely one of the country's most noted liberals and was the founder of the ADA. Several years ago, he appeared on the University of Chicago's Roundtable broadcast entitled "What is Communism?" Schlesinger said this, and I quote, "Surely the class struggle is going on in America. I would agree completely with the communists on that." Schlesinger was then asked, "Do you mean capitalism is dead everywhere except in the U.S.?" Schlesinger replied, "It is dead. It died of itself. There is much too much the Marxists used to say about capitalism containing the seeds of its own destruction."

Now this talk about the "class war" and about capitalism "containing the seeds of its own destruction" is pure communist propaganda originated by Karl Marx. There isn't any class war in America except that which the communists foment. Capitalism creates the seeds of its own regeneration and it is socialism that contains the seeds of its own destruction. After WWII, the countries which went to freedom, to free enterprise, such as Germany and Japan, today are enjoying the highest standards of living and the greatest prosperity those countries have ever known, whereas the countries that went to socialism, like England, have had a declining standard of living and continued austerity in spite of massive transfusions of American aid.

Now, the liberals, it's because of their acceptance of the fundamental premises of socialism that the liberals have a deplorable record of being deceived by the communists. It's a matter of historical fact that the liberals supported the communists in Spain in 1936, the communists in Poland in 1945, the communists in China in 1948, the communists in Cuba in 1958, and the communists in the Congo in 1961. The liberals fell for the lie that the Soviet Union was a peace-loving democracy. One of the country's leading liberals, a very smart man, was our ambassador to Soviet Russia called Joseph Davies. In his best-selling book, called *Mission to Moscow*, Mr. Davies wrote, "Stalin is decent and clean-living. A child would like to sit in his lap, and a dog would sidle up to him." And on June 11, 1948, a very prominent liberal in our country declared, "I like old Joe Stalin; he's a decent fellow." Now, the truth of the matter is that Stalin was so indecent, and his crimes were so foul that even the "Butcher of Budapest" couldn't stand having his body around the Kremlin and he had to have it disinterred and thrown in the river.

But the liberals were fooled again by the Chinese Reds; they called them "agrarian reformers," Jeffersonian and democrat. And they didn't learn ten years later. They told us that Castro was an "agrarian reformer," a sincere idealist. The liberals like Edward R. Murrow and Jack Paar were completely taken in. *The New York Times* told us that Castro was a "Robin Hood," and the "Abraham Lincoln" of Cuba. And Ed Sullivan put Castro on a Sunday evening television show and called him the "George Washington of Cuba." Last December 2, Castro went on the air and boasted that he has been a dedicated communist ever since 1953. But he acted in a foxy way in order to deceive the liberals whose support he needed.

Well, last November 8, President Kennedy said, "If the Soviet Union fooled us once, it's their fault. If they fool us twice, it's our fault." But the fact is that the liberals have been fooled again and again and again, and still they do not learn because the liberals today are supporting the communist takeover of the Congo, and their policy is to get the anti-communists in the Congo to join in a coalition government with known communists in key positions in the name of coalition, and anyone who has studied history knows that coalition with the communists is always a prelude to communist takeover.

Now today we are engaged in a life-and-death struggle with the international communist conspiracy, a struggle which requires the patriotic efforts of all Americans. Last November in Seattle, President Kennedy said that we face "the burden of a long twilight struggle." Well, now, I didn't understand his choice of words, because even my three-year-old daughter knows that twilight is followed by a long night. And it will soon be a dark age from which civilization may never recover if we do not substitute this defeatist attitude of the liberals with the will to achieve victory over communism. In order to do this, it is necessary for every American to learn what the communists' tactics are so that we can recognize them, whether we see them on a television screen or in the magazines or on the movies or wherever. Because of the practical matter, it doesn't make much difference whether the line is being spread by a communist, a socialist, a liberal or a dupe. If someone sets fire to your house, does it really matter whether it is a professional arsonist or just a fool playing with matches? The damage is going to be the same.

Then let us learn what the communist tactics are. Here are the top ones of the present time:

First, to smear all anti-communists in line with the directive laid down on December 5, 1960, by the Communist Party, and since then laid relentlessly in the communist press.

Two, to promote disarmament and the continued suspension of nuclear tests by the United States.

Third, to capture the minds of our youth by communist fronts on the campuses of our universities and by communist propaganda which is today pouring into our country at the rate of 15 million pieces per year carried free by our Post Office.

Four, to discredit the House on Un-American Activities Committee and the Senate Internal Security Subcommittee.

Fifth, to shore up the communists' and socialists' regime by United States foreign aid to such Soviet satellites as Tito and to such so-called "neutralists" as Indonesia and Ghana.

Six, to promote trade and cultural exchanges with communist countries.

Seventh, to dismantle the remaining rules and regulations protecting our internal security.

And eighth, to use the slogans that "colonialism is bad" in order to drive the West from Africa, Asia, and even Latin America, even through stealing the Panama Canal from the United States. If we recognize the communists' tactics, we will then be able to say that we are not in the "twilight," but we are in the dawn of a great victory over communists.

Those doctors and others who have studied biology and done experiments with frogs and mice in the laboratory may be interested in an experiment which was performed for me by a doctor friend of mine by the name of Walters. This is an experiment which illustrates scientifically a truth which we must all grasp if we are to protect our freedoms and independence. If we would learn this lesson well, this experiment may become as famous as Franklin's kite. One day, Dr. Walters put a big kettle of water on the stove and turned on the heat, and we sat there in the kitchen and discussed world affairs until the kettle of water was boiling cheerfully. And then he reached into a pail he had brought with him and brought out a struggling frog and, with some effort, dropped the frog into the pot of boiling water. Instantaneously, there was a great explosion of boiling water as the frog jumped out and hopped across the room and took refuge under the icebox. And then Dr. Walters poured the boiling water down the drain and refilled the kettle with cold water. He reached into his pail and pulled out a second frog and dropped it into the cold water. And then he turned the heat on low, and we sat there and discussed world affairs. And finally there were little wisps of steam coming up in the kettle, and the frog did a little bit of kicking (but not very much). And we talked on, and finally when the kettle was boiling, Dr. Walters said, "Now the moment of revelation is upon us." For we looked in the kettle, and there we saw lying there one very dead frog. "Now," Dr. Walters said, "The moral of this experiment is this: the frog dropped into the boiling water has got enough sense to jump out fast. But the frog that is dropped in cold water can be cooked to death before he ever realizes he's in serious trouble."

If the communists landed their armies in New York City and started marching west, every man in this room would be on his feet to go out and protect his home and his country. We must be ever vigilant to make sure that our enemies do not achieve by gradualism, by propaganda, and by perversion, what they could never achieve by force. It needs the patriotic effort of every American if that country is to continue to be what Abraham Lincoln called it: "The last best hope on earth."

# 1987

# We The People

O ur Constitution should be in the Guinness Book of World Records as the oldest and longest-lasting constitution in all the world's history! September 17, 1987 marks the 200th birthday of the signing of our Constitution.

Today we will explore for a little while:

WHY the United States Constitution is the fountainhead of our great liberties—religious, political, and economic;

HOW our Constitution enabled America to grow and prosper, becoming the most powerful country in the world, while at the same time preserving individual freedoms; and

WHAT is in the Constitution that caused these happy results.

First, let's discuss what America was like in the years preceding the writing of the Constitution.

On July 4, 1776, 56 brave men signed the Declaration of Independence, an inspired document written largely by Thomas Jefferson. The Declaration founded our new nation on an entirely new principle: that individual rights, including life and liberty, come from God, our Creator, NOT from the state; that the purpose of government is to secure these God-given individual rights; and that government derives its powers from the consent of the governed.

For the first time, government was proclaimed servant, rather than master. The signers of the Declaration appealed directly to God to justify their right to exercise sovereign power in an independent nation.

The Declaration of Independence has five references to God—God as Creator of all men, God as the source of all rights, God as the supreme lawmaker, God as the world's

197

supreme judge, and God as our patron and protector. The Declaration proclaims God's existence as a "self-evident" truth which requires no further discussion or debate. The Declaration is the religious and philosophical foundation.

The Declaration of Independence was followed by our eight-year War for Independence against England. The fate of our nation hung in the balance many times during those years of bitter fighting. The American patriots endured cold winters, without adequate clothing or pay, sustained by the tremendous personal leadership of Washington.

When the war was finally won, and George Washington accepted the surrender of Cornwallis at Yorktown, the next task was to negotiate a peace treaty with Great Britain. Fortunately, America had peacemakers who equaled the vision, determination and perseverance of the patriots who had risked their lives, their fortunes and their sacred honor on the field of battle. Peacemakers understood there was no substitute for victory.

Our three negotiators were John Adams, (who later became our second President), John Jay (who later became our

first Chief Justice), and Benjamin Franklin (our most
distinguished diplomat). Their three years of negotiations
produced the Treaty of Paris signed on September 3,
1783—the most successful treaty we ever signed. John
Adams hailed this Treaty as "one of the most important
political events that ever happened on this globe."

The goal of our negotiators was not peace, but was
perpetual American independence. Our negotiators knew that
our independence would always be in jeopardy if Britain were
allowed to keep troops in Maine, South Carolina, Georgia, and
if the British or Spanish were allowed to remain in the area
west of the Alleghenies to the Mississippi River.

So our negotiators held fast to a no-compromise, hard-
line determination to pursue victory at the peace table—and
they won. By the Treaty of Paris, England not only recognized
the United States as "free, sovereign and independent," but
recognized our mastery over territory twice as large as the
original 13 colonies. By the stroke of a pen, America was no
longer just a confederation of 13 states along the Atlantic coast,
but was a territory that stretched to Canada on the north, the

Mississippi River on the west, and Florida on the south. Treaty of Paris boundaries gave us the space to grow.

AFTER we had declared our independence and freedom, AFTER we had won our independence and freed America in a bitter and bloody war, and AFTER we had persuaded the European powers to recognize our independence and freedom plus space to grow, the next question was, what would we do with our independence and freedom? What kind of government?

The American government, which functioned during the Revolutionary War, was set up under the Articles of Confederation. That first government was not adequate to cope with the problems of war, peace, or commerce. No executive. No courts. No tax. It had no power to regulate interstate or foreign trade.

In a great speech made 50 years later, President John Quincy Adams explained that the principal problem with the Articles of Confederation was that they departed from the philosophical foundations of the Declaration of Independence. The defects of the Confederation were vices of the structure, NOT of the men who administered it. The Articles of

Confederation designed a federation of sovereign, jealous states, rather than a national government to protect the God-given rights of free people. As the years passed after the Treaty of Paris, 1783, 1784, 1785, it became increasingly apparent that we desperately needed a government to preserve the freedom and independence we had won. At George Washington's residence, Mount Vernon, in 1785, our founding patriots began to discuss the need to revise the Articles.

The Virginia Legislature called for a trade conference to meet in Annapolis, Maryland in September 1786. Delegates came from only five states. The Annapolis Convention accomplished only one thing. James Madison of Virginia met with Alexander Hamilton of New York, and they decided to ask the Continental Congress to call a convention of the 13 states to revise the Articles.

On May 25, 1787, the convention opened at Independence Hall in Philadelphia. Fifty-five delegates representing 12 states eventually attended. They passed a resolution to keep their meetings closed and secret, and then buckled down to serious work in Independence Hall. The 55 men who met and debated that hot summer in Philadelphia, from May 25 to September 17, were men of extraordinary vision, wisdom, and commitment. They had a shared sense of mission and of political values. Thomas Jefferson, called them "an assembly of demigods."

The steady hand at the helm was General George Washington, who was unanimously elected convention president. No speeches, but personal leadership, prestige as commander kept the argumentative delegates on course, leading onward to their glorious goal. Washington stated his approach to the task in these words. "If to please the people, we offer that which we ourselves disapprove how can we afterwards defend our work? Let us raise a standard to which wise and honest can repair."

The senior citizen at the convention was Benjamin Franklin—diplomat, inventor, business success, and world-renowned statesman.

After the first month of convention sessions had produced little progress, Ben Franklin made a speech to warn his fellow delegates that, if they failed to produce a workable constitution, future generations might conclude that mankind is incapable of self-government, and then leave government "to chance, to conquest, and to war." Dr. Franklin urged the delegates to pray daily for the success of their mission. He said, "I have lived a long time, and the longer I live the more convincing proofs I see of this truth: that God governs in the affairs of men ... I firmly believe this, and I also believe that without His concurring aid, we shall succeed in this political building no better than the builders of Babel."

The Philadelphia convention was a gathering of very young men; the average age of the delegates, even including Ben Franklin at 81, was only 41. But they were men who were well-read in the great books of social, political and economic theory, such as the Bible, the French philosopher Montesquieu, the English writer John Locke, and the economist Adam Smith. Twenty-three had been soldiers. Both a study of history and firsthand experience had taught the Founding Fathers about the structural defects of all previous forms of government.

The delegates were sent to Philadelphia for the express purpose of revising the Articles of Confederation. But one delegate from Virginia, who lived in a beautiful home in Orange County called Montpelier, arrived with the vision of forming an entirely new government. James Madison believed that the Articles of Confederation were hopelessly defective, and that they should be completely replaced by an entirely different constitution. On June 19, Madison made a moving speech in which he argued that the convention must come up with a "Constitution for the Ages."

James Madison was only 36 years old, but he already had experience in constitution writing. He had served in the Virginia convention which drafted the state constitution, and he was the author of the religious-freedom clause which guaranteed "liberty of conscience for all." His role in Philadelphia, as the principal architect of our new and unique American system of government, earned for James Madison the title, Father of the Constitution.

The Commission on the Bicentennial of the United States Constitution hopes that every American will read and study the Constitution this year until its words are familiar and dear to every citizen. Today we have time only to outline the basic principles of the Constitution and the structure of the government and Constitution created.

The first principle of our Constitution is the sovereignty of the people. The Founding Fathers proclaimed this in the first words of the Constitution: "We the People of the United States ... do ordain and establish this Constitution for the United States of America." The unique American concept of political power is that government is the servant of the people, not their master. Different from Magna Carta, in which a reluctant king was forced to give up some of his rights. The "We the People" theory of our Constitution is based on the same as the Declaration of Independence.

The second principle is our reliance on a written Constitution. Our Founding Fathers wanted and gave us a government of laws, not of men. A government whose powers and limitations were defined on paper for all to see. They rejected the British notion of an unwritten Constitution which can change with Parliamentary majorities or judicial whim. Our written Constitution was proclaimed as "the supreme Law of the Land" in Article 6.

The third principle of our Constitution is the structure of government which we call the Separation of Powers. Our Constitution separated the powers of government so that each section can serve as a check on the others, and so that no one section can become powerful. The reasoning behind this is clear. While the people should grant enough power to government so it can effectively function, we the people really don't trust government—and so we must section off government into competing branches, with each functioning as a check.

James Madison, one of the principal architects of our Constitution, believed that the best way to achieve the twin goals of liberty and justice was in this original institutional design created by the Constitution. By "contriving the interior structure of the government" in a particular way, Madison argued, "its several constituent parts may, by their mutual relations, be the means of keeping each other in their proper places."

Accordingly, the power of government was first divided between the federal government and the states. The federal government was given certain enumerated powers, such as powers over national defense and interstate commerce, with all the remaining powers reserved to the states and to the people. For example, family law, education, and control over cities were areas of law not given to the federal government, but reserved to the states and the people.

Secondly, the power granted to the federal government was divided again into three branches: the legislative, the executive, and the judicial, each with its prescribed list of enumerated powers. As James Madison put it, the "preservation of liberty requires that the three great departments of power should be separate and distinct." The functioning of our Government does not depend on the goodness of those who hold the power, but depends on the institutional restraints imposed on their power.

Article I of the Constitution grants "all" the federal government's legislative power to the Congress, which meets now in the United States Capitol Building in Washington, D.C. Article I states very specifically what Congress may do, and what it may not do.

Article II defines the powers and duties of the executive branch, headed by the President.

Article III creates the judicial branch, headed by

the Supreme Court, which meets in one of the most beautiful buildings in the world. Under the Supreme Court, there are now hundreds of district courts.

The Separation of Powers concept is entirely different from parliamentary systems, such as the British, where the executive and legislative branches are combined. Congress may not fire the President, as the British Parliament can fire the Prime Minister. The President may NOT dissolve Congress, as the British Prime Minister can dissolve Parliament and call a new election. The Founding Fathers emphatically opposed the President having that power.

Members of Congress may NOT serve in executive branch offices, such as the Cabinet. That would violate the separation principle. James Madison argued that the accumulation of legislative, executive, and judicial powers in the same hands, is "the very definition of tyranny."

Now look at the ingenious and interlacing network of checks and balances that function among the three branches.

Congress makes all the laws, but they do not take effect unless signed by the President. The President can veto any act of Congress, but the Congress can pass the law over his veto by a two-thirds vote. The President is Commander in Chief of the Armed Services, but only Congress may declare war. The President can sign treaties, but they do not have any validity unless ratified by two-thirds of the Senators. The Founding Fathers were very familiar with the way the British king had exclusive power to make treaties, and they did not want the American President to.

The Supreme Court has the power of judicial review. It may not legislate or execute laws or engage in policymaking, but the Court can nullify an unconstitutional law. All federal court judges enjoy life tenure, but Congress has the power to take away or limit the jurisdiction of lower federal courts and the appellate jurisdiction of the Supreme Court.

The fourth principle of the Constitution is the concept of limited government—that the Federal Government enjoys only the powers that are listed, and that here are many things government may not do at all. The philosophical foundation of the Declaration of Independence and the Constitution is that individual rights come from God, that sovereignty lies in the people and, therefore, government enjoys only those limited powers which the people give it.

The purpose of the Constitution was to list specific powers of the federal government, with the clear understanding that everything else remained in the hands of the people and the several states. Most important, government officials were never to exercise enough power to trample on our God-given unalienable rights. This principle makes the Constitution itself a bill of rights.

The fifth principle of the Constitution is economic freedom for every individual, combined with the concept that our nation is one economic unit. The opportunity to engage freely in any business, trade, occupation or profession was one of the most important liberties, along with right to own property and to make contracts. James Madison stated that the security of property was one of the "primary objects of civil society." Alexander Hamilton said that a principal object of their endeavors was "the prosperity of commerce."

Both Madison and Hamilton believed that the right of private property ranks with the most important personal liberties. The right of property means that people can work hard and retain their earnings for themselves, their families and their children, except for taxes justly and fairly imposed. But it means much more than that. Only a nation that enjoys economic freedom can enjoy political freedom. Only if you are secure in the ownership of your property, and the right to choose your occupation, can you speak your mind and vote your choice without fear.

At the same time, Article I gave the federal government the power "to regulate commerce among the several States." This Commerce Clause in the Constitution gave us one economic system in which every farmer and every craftsman is encouraged to produce by the certainty that he will have free access to every market in America, and no one state can erect trade barriers against another.

Hamilton said that the Constitution would create "one great American system," forever independent of European economic control. It took Western Europe until after World War II to understand the "common market."

This combination of powers given and NOT given to the new government opened the door to economic growth and abundance such as the world had never seen before. Our system of economic freedom unleashed the productivity and resourcefulness of Americans, and started our nation on its climb to a prosperity that is the envy of the world.

The sixth principle of the Constitution is representative government under procedures and restraints specified in the Constitution. The Separation of Powers principle mandates separate and distinct terms for each federal elective office: a four-year term for the President and Vice President, a six-year term for Senators, and a two-year term for members of the House of Representatives. Each office must be voted on separately. The President may not run as a "ticket."

The Electoral College, which is our system of electing American Presidents, was spelled out in Article II. It is an ingenious method of adapting representative government to the separation of Powers guidelines. The Electoral College is the only occasion in our political process when 50 percent of the entire nation must agree on something or someone. It, therefore, provides a basis for the national leadership our country needs. The Electoral College is the only function of our national government that is performed outside of Washington, D.C. No Senator, Congressman, or federal official is permitted to be an elector.

The separation of the Congress into the Senate and the House was an inspired division of power which balances the interests of the big population states and the small population states. Every state, no matter what its population, has two Senators, now making a total of 100 for the 50 states. The 435 Representatives in the House are apportioned according to each state's population; and the Constitution requires they be reapportioned every 10 years.

All tax bills must originate in the House of Representatives, the body where every member must run for reelection every two years. The Founding Fathers knew that oppressive taxes were the main cause of the Revolution. The two-year term of Congressmen is one of our greatest guarantees of freedom. James Madison persuasively argued that "frequency of elections is the cornerstone ... of free government."

The Founding Fathers' experience with England, where Parliament was all-powerful, had convinced them that, as Madison said, the legislature has a tendency to extend the "sphere of its activity" and to draw "all power into its impetuous vortex." The different terms of office and separate elections for the President, and for Senators and Representatives, were one of the ways to limit the power of Congress.

The writers of the Constitution could not solve all our nation's problems. They could not solve the problem of slavery. But the Founding Fathers did give us a structure of government, and a procedure for amending the Constitution, under which those could eventually be solved.

The Constitution was as perfect as humans could make it. The British Prime Minister, William Gladstone, later called it, "the greatest piece of work ever struck off at a given time by the brain and purpose of man." The great French writer, Alexis de Tocqueville, pronounced it "the most perfect Federal Constitution that ever existed."

When the task of writing the Constitution was completed, then came the moment of truth. Would enough delegates sign the document to send it to the states?

On the last day of the Constitutional Convention, wise old Ben Franklin rose to say, "I doubt whether any other convention we can obtain may be able to make a better Constitution . ... It astonishes me to find this system approaching so near to perfection as it does ... I wish that every member of the convention who may still have objections to it, would, with me on this occasion, doubt a little of his own infallibility, and to make manifest our unanimity, put his name to this instrument."

On September 17, 1787, the Constitution of the United States was signed by 39 delegates representing 12 states.

Pointing to the carving on the back of George Washington's chair, Benjamin Franklin said, "I have ... often, in the course of the session, ... looked at that [sun] behind the President without being able to tell whether it was rising or setting. But now at length, I have the happiness to know that it is a rising and not a setting sun."

When the news rang out that the Constitution had been signed, many people referred to it as a miracle.

In writing to the Marquis de Lafayette in 1788, George Washington wrote that it was "little short of a miracle that the delegates from so many different states should unite in forming a system of national government."

James Madison wrote to Thomas Jefferson, who was in France, that it was "impossible to consider the degree of concord which ultimately prevailed as less than a miracle." It is "impossible" not to perceive "a finger of that Almighty hand" in the writing.

Then, the ratification battle began. Some distinguished patriots opposed it on states' rights grounds, others because of the omission of a Bill of Rights.

To promote ratification of the Constitution, James Madison, Alexander Hamilton, and John Jay wrote 85 articles explaining its terms. These articles, published under the name The Federalist Papers, are the most valuable source for determining the meaning of the Constitution.

By January 1788, Delaware, Pennsylvania, New Jersey, Georgia, and Connecticut had ratified. The Constitution became official when the ninth state, New Hampshire, ratified it in June 1788.

On February 4, 1789, George Washington was unanimously elected our first President. He took his oath of office on April 30, 1789, and our new government started to function. We had achieved the first purpose of the Constitution: "To form a more perfect Union."

As soon as the new government was formed, the first order of business was to write and ratify a Bill of Rights. Several of the states might not have ratified the Constitution at all except on the promise of a Bill of Rights.

At the Constitutional Convention in Philadelphia, the Founding Fathers had thought that a Bill of Rights was not necessary for two reasons. First, the Constitution itself, from beginning to end, is a declaration of rights. Secondly, under our theory that government possesses only those limited powers granted to it by the Constitution, the Federal Government should never have any power to interfere with individual rights anyway.

But "we the people" saw this matter differently. The people feared, based on their past experience, that government officials might twist the meanings of words so as to deprive them of their rights. James Madison, who was elected to the first House of Representatives, immediately undertook the task of writing the first Amendments: freedom of religion, speech, press, assembly, and property, and the rights to keep and bear arms, trial by jury, and due process. Ten Amendments, known as the Bill of Rights, were ratified by 1791.

In the next two centuries, only 16 more Amendments were added to the Constitution. That is tremendous proof of the near-perfection of the original document, its structural soundness, and its vitality even though our population today is 80 times what it was 200 years ago.

Six of those Amendments extended voting rights— questions not foreseen by the Founding Fathers because they expected all elections to be controlled by the states, rather than by the federal government.

The Founding Fathers were writing a Constitution NOT merely for their times but for the future forever, no matter how large our nation. James Madison predicted, in a letter in the 1820s: "We have framed a Constitution that will probably be around when there are 196 million people."

For example, the language of the Constitution is completely sex-neutral. From the day it was signed, women have been eligible to serve in every position.

The original, signed Constitution of the United States is preserved in special cases in the National Archives Building in Washington, D.C. It can be seen and treasured by everyone, and school children should study it.

In a remarkable speech on the Constitution 50 years after the Constitution went into effect, President John Quincy Adams reminded us that our wonderful American blessings are the result of our adherence to "the principles of the Declaration of Independence, practically interwoven in the Constitution of the United States." He exhorted us to "Lay up these principles, then, in your hearts, and in your souls. Bind them for signs upon your hands, that they may be as frontlets between your eyes. Teach them to your children, speaking of them when sitting in your houses, when walking by the way, when lying down and when rising up. Write them upon the doorplates of your houses, and upon your gates. Cling to them as to the issues of life. Adhere to them as to the cords of your eternal salvation. So may your children's children ... after another century of experience under our national Constitution, celebrate it again in the full enjoyment of all its blessings."

That is not just an old-fashioned view from the last century. Listen to the words of one of the most popular writers of our current era, James Michener. "The writing of the Constitution of the United States is an act of such genius that philosophers still wonder at its accomplishment and envy its results ... They fashioned a nearly perfect instrument of government ... What this mix of men did was create a miracle in which every American should take pride. Their decision to divide the power of the government into three parts—Legislative, Executive, Judicial—was a master stroke. The accumulated wisdom of mankind speaks in this Constitution."

## March 27, 1979
## Orlando, Florida
## The Positive Woman's Movement

G ood morning friends. The subject assigned today is, indeed, an important one: the women's movement and family life.

It is important that we first of all define the term. I would not agree that there is just the women's movement. In order to make sure we know what we are talking about, I will first of all describe what I think could be more appropriately called the women's liberation movement. It could be defined as the movement of women who have, in a general way, been working for the Equal Rights Amendment.

This movement was born in the mid-1960s with the publication of Betty Friedan's book, *The Feminine Mystique.* This movement accomplished the task of getting the Equal

Rights Amendment through Congress in 1972. It reached its peak in November 1977 in Houston at the National Conference of the Commission on International Women's Year. Since that date, it's no longer a nebulous thing. It is a very precise movement that can be definitely defined with particular people and particular goals.

Participating in that Houston Conference were all the leaders of the women's liberation movement. These included the head of the National Organization for Women (NOW), the head of the Women's Political Caucus, the head of ERAmerica (the lobbying group for the ERA), the head of the Gay Task Force, the person who put the ERA through the Senate, the person who put ERA though the House, Gloria Steinem, and Bella Abzug was the chairman. These were all presidential appointees, and they gathered in Houston. They had $5 million of federal funds and they passed twenty-five resolutions, which represent the goals of the women's liberation movement.

The four "hot button" issues, the term used by *Newsweek* magazine, their most important goals, were ratification of the Equal Rights Amendment, government-funded abortion, lesbian privileges to be recognized with the same dignity as husbands and wives and with the right to teach in schools, and massive, universal, federal child care, which *Time* magazine estimated would cost us an additional $25 billion a year. There were other resolutions, too, but the four "hot button" issues were admitted by everybody—the media plus both sides—as being the main ones.

These are the goals and those are the personalities of the women's liberation movement in our country today. It is my belief, based on working with this movement for quite a number of years, that the movement is having an adverse effect on family life, that it is a major cause of divorce today, and that it is highly detrimental to our country and to our families. For a woman to function effectively in the family, it is necessary for her to believe in the worth of her position, to have a certain amount of self-esteem, to believe that her task as wife and mother is worthy, is honorable, is useful, and is fulfilling. The fundamental attitude by the women's liberation movement takes all that away from women. I have listened to thousands of their speeches, and basically those speeches inculcate in women a negative attitude toward life, toward the family, toward their country, and most of all toward themselves. It was best summed up in an advertisement developed by the principal women's liberation organization, the National Organization for Women. It was run as a spot announcement on many television stations and as ads in many magazines and newspapers. This advertisement shows a darling, curly-headed child. The caption under the picture is, "This normal, healthy child was born with a handicap. It was born female."

Think about that. That is the startling assumption of the woman's liberation movement. That somebody—it isn't clear who, God or the establishment or a conspiracy of male chauvinist pigs—has dealt women a foul blow by making them female; that it is up to society to remedy these centuries of oppression, of bondage, even of slavery. Women are told that they are not even persons in our society. They are told that they are second-class citizens. I have given speeches where women have been picketing up and down outside, wearing placards saying, "I am a second-class citizen." I feel so sorry for women who are deliberately inculcating this inferiority complex. Women are not second-class citizens in our society. Whatever women may have been hundreds of years ago, in other lands, or in other countries, that is not the condition of women in our country today. The thesis of the speeches that women's liberation movement speakers are giving runs basically like this. "Sister, when you wake up in the morning, the cards are stacked against you. You won't get a job, and if you get one, it won't be a good one. You'll never be paid what you're really worth. You won't be promoted as you deserve to be. You simply will never get a fair break in our society. And if you get married, your husband will treat you like a servant, like a chattel"—that's one of their favorite words—"and life is nothing but a bunch of dirty diapers and dirty dishes."

It's no wonder that women have problems when they listen to that line. The women's liberation movement literature is the greatest put-down of women that anything could possibly be. It's difficult to pick yourself up off the floor after you have listened to those tirades about how women are kept in bondage and enslaved, and how the home is a cage or a prison from which women must be liberated. This line creates a natural hostility between men and women. No longer are men people with whom we work in harmony. Men are the enemy who must make it up to us for these centuries of injustice.

Whatever lowly status women may endure in other lands, that is not the situation of American women. It is also true that nobody in this world who wakes up in the morning with a chip on your shoulder, whether it is man or woman, is going to have a happy or fulfilling life, or get ahead in this world.

This is not to say that there aren't any problems. The world is full of problems. I don't know anybody who doesn't have problems. Women face all kinds of problems: husbands out of a job, handicapped children, senile parents, or not enough money. The world is full of problems. But you don't solve your problems by waking up in the morning with a chip on your shoulder, believing and telling yourself hour after hour that you've been oppressed, and that it is up to somebody to remedy years of injustice.

After having flattened women by spreading this negative attitude, the women's liberation movement then comes along and offers its solution. The solution can be best described as the "new narcissism." You remember the story of Narcissus: the Greek youth who fell in love with his own image in the reflecting pool and finally died of unrequited desire. The women's liberation movement teaches women this fundamental approach to life: "Seek your own self-fulfillment over every other value." It's a free country for those who choose to establish their scale of values that way. Some women make that choice, and they are free to do so if that is what they want. But I simply have to tell women that that attitude, that choice of goals, is not compatible with a happy marriage. It is not compatible with a successful family life and it is not compatible with motherhood.

In order to live in harmony in family life, with a man who's been brought up in another environment, you have to make social compromises, and most of us think that marriage is worth the price.

Motherhood must be a self-sacrificing role, a role of dedication and service. The mother must be able to subordinate her self-fulfillment and her desire for a career to the well-being of her children so that she can answer her child's call any hour of the day or night. This is what marriage and motherhood are all about, and it is not compatible with the dogmas of the women's liberation movement.

The women's liberation movement preaches that the greatest oppression of women is that women get pregnant and men don't get pregnant, and so women must be relieved of this oppression! The second greatest oppression of women, according to the liberation movement, is that society expects mothers to look after their babies, that society reduces women to this menial, tedious, tiresome, confining, repetitious chore of looking after babies.

Well, I suppose it's all in your point of view. Many of us believe that the ability to participate in the creation of human life is the great gift that God gave to women. The task of taking care of babies, despite its tedious drudgery, is better than most of the jobs of the world. Women should find out how exhausting most of the rest of the jobs of the world are. Besides, a mother has something to show for her efforts after twenty years: You've got a living, breathing human being, a good citizen, a wonderful human being you've given to this world.

But the women's movement is causing wives with relatively good families to walk out. Women's lib is a dogma that is especially contagious among women in their forties and fifties after their children are in school. Wives who "catch" the disease of women's liberation are walking out on marriage—

not because of the traditional problems in marriage such as alcohol, or money, or adultery, but just to seek their own self-fulfillment.

I speak almost every week on college campuses and I see these abandoned teenagers. Young women come up to me and say, "My mother has left. What can you say to my mother, who has brought up four children and now thinks her whole life is wasted?" The women who "catch" women's liberation are walking out. It makes no difference whether they're northern and eastern liberal homes or southern and western conservative homes. Once they get this message, they go out into emptiness, abandoning their families.

This women's liberation dogma is also very contagious among young college women. They have bought a large part of it. The biggest thing that hits you on the college campuses today is that the educated young women of our nation are rejecting marriage and motherhood. Most important, they're rejecting motherhood. They're saying that if they have a baby, they don't want it to interfere with their careers. I have young men coming to me now saying that they want to marry a young woman, but she tells them very frankly, "If we have a baby,

I'm not going to let that baby interfere with my career. I see nothing the matter with putting the baby in some child-care facility at the age of three or four weeks." Remember, this is not a matter of need.

These are not hungry people. These are a class of women who expect to have degrees but they don't want that baby to interfere with their careers. Of course, my answer to those young men is, "Forget her." A woman who is unwilling to take care of her own baby is a pathetic sight, and there's nothing in marriage for a man to have a relationship like that. This is what the women's liberation movement is doing to the young women of our nation.

There is another women's movement. You don't hear much about it but I believe it is more powerful. It is the Positive Woman's Movement. The woman who knows who she is. The Positive Woman is not searching for her identity. She knows God made her, she knows why she's here, and she has her scale of values in order. This movement was born in 1972 when some of us realized we had to protect ourselves against the takeaway of the legal rights of the homemaker that was embodied in the Equal Rights Amendment. This

movement showed itself at the marvelous Pro-Family Rally in
Houston in 1977 where 15,000 people came at their own
expense—not like the other one where people came at the
taxpayers' expense. Our movement of Positive Women came
of age on March 22, 1979, in Washington, D.C., when we
celebrated, at a marvelous dinner in Washington, the expiration
of the seven years that was set as the time period for
ratification of the Equal Rights Amendment.

Our Positive Women are not seeking their own self-
fulfillment as the highest value, as the women's liberation
movement tries to teach women. Our Positive Women are
dedicated to service, to faith and trust in God, to the family,
and to this great country that we have been fortunate enough to
live in. We are not seeking to get our bit at the price of taking
benefits away from others, as the woman's liberation
movement is doing. We have taken on these great odds,
believing, as we are told in II Chronicles, "Be not afraid, nor
dismayed by reason of the great multitude, for the battle is not
yours but God's."

We have fought the greatest political forces that
anybody has ever fought in our country in this century. We

have won, with God's help, because we are Positive Women. We don't wake up in the morning mad at anybody. We have women who are talented, articulate, capable. We have lady legislators and successful career women. We have some who are solely successful career women, others who are wives and mothers but who are also successful in an auxiliary career. The great thing about woman's role is that she can have different careers at different times in her life. But our Positive Women have their scale of values in order: no matter what they may seek for their own self-fulfillment, they know that the family is more important. Our women are, I believe, the greatest positive force in our country today. We believe that we can do great things. Now that we move into the more positive phase of our activity, we will work for the restoration of the family unit, which is coming apart at the seams in many areas. We want to show women how, in this great country, women can do whatever they want and have all kinds of exciting lives. But for a woman to be a successful wife and mother, during that period of her life, marriage and motherhood must come first over selfish values.

In conclusion, I share with you the comment attributed to a French writer who traveled our country in another century and wrote many commentaries which are still studied in our schools. When he came to the conclusion of his travels, Alexis de Tocqueville wrote, "I sought for the greatness and genius of America in her commodious harbors and ample rivers, but it was not there. I sought for the greatness of America in her fertile lands and boundless prairies, but it was not there. It was not until I went into the churches of America and found her pulpits aflame with righteousness that I understood the secret of her genius and her power. America is great because America is good, and if America ever ceases to be good, she will cease to be great."

The Positive Women of America are pledging themselves to do our part to make sure that America continues to be good.

## November 19, 1977
## Houston, Texas
## God, Family, and Country

T hank you Mr. Chairman and good afternoon dear friends. There are many differences between *this* meeting and the one in that other hall today. We started out by offering a prayer and I think you should know that at that *other* meeting they didn't have a prayer ... they just started out with a moment of silence for fear they would offend many of their members who were present. I'm very proud that they excluded me from that convention. And I'm here where we're *not ashamed* and *not afraid* to ask God's blessing on this crowd assembled here today.

But I do thank all of you for coming and for giving us here on the platform the thrill of seeing this marvelous crowd. I am informed that there are 15,000 inside and several thousand more who have unfortunately been turned away.

At the very first meeting of the Commission on International Women's Year, they adopted an official resolution: To urge and push for ratification of the Equal Rights Amendment as their highest priority. They resolved, "to do all in their capacity to see that the Equal Rights Amendment is ratified at the earliest possible moment." Now when you have $5 million to spend, all in your capacity is a lot indeed. I can tell you that if we had $5 million we would've buried it five years ago.

The Commission on International Women's Year is a costly mistake at the taxpayer's expense. The whole thing was designed as a media event; a charade to go through the motions of these phony state conferences and national conferences in order to pass resolutions that were pre-written and pre-packaged a year and a half ago and published in June of 1976. And then, after it was all over, to tell the Congress and the state legislators that *this* is what American women want. By coming here today, you have shown that that is *not* what American women want.

Several years ago a study was made about the Equal Rights Amendment at the Drake Law School in Iowa. And they concluded that if the Equal Rights Amendment were ever ratified, it would encourage the legislators, and the state, and the courts, to adopt a wildly permissive role, which would have the effect of driving the homemaker out of the home. This is what certain people want.

And why would it do that? It would do that, first of all, because it would make unconstitutional any state law which makes it the obligation of the husband to support his wife and children. These laws are basic to the institution of the family. These are the laws which give to the wife her legal right to be in the home. These are the laws which give to the children their right to have a mother in the home. Some people *do* want this. The Equal Rights Amendment proponents *do want* that obligation to be sex-equal. They *do want* to take the wife out of the home. They *do want* to get them in the workforce because then this will greatly increase the taxes and the bureaucracy of the federal government.

Section 2 of the Equal Rights Amendment gives the whole enforcement power on the Equal Rights Amendment to the federal government. Why in the world would anybody want to give the Washington politicians and bureaucrats and judges more power than they now have, when they can't *possibly* solve the problems they have already?

The Equal Rights Amendment says you cannot discriminate on account of sex. And if you want to deny a marriage license to a man and a man, or deny a homosexual the right to teach in the schools, or adopt children, it is on account of sex that you would deny it, and that would be unconstitutional under the ERA.

We reject the anti-family goals of the equal rights amendment and the International Women's Year. Contrary to their radical resolutions, the American people and the American women do not want the ERA. They do not want abortion. They do not want lesbian privileges. And they do not want universal childcare in the hands of the government.

When I look out at this crowd today, I know that you have the energy and the dedication to *defeat* this assault on the family. If you cared enough to come here today, I know that you *can* do it. You can turn back this tide all across the country. If you stay with us, the Equal Rights Amendment *will die* 16 months from Tuesday.

In order to have held the line for the last five years against the tremendous odds of White House lobbying, federal government expenditure, prominent people, and big money, we *had* to have somebody on our side who is more powerful than the President of the United States.

But we need your help and we can have another party on March 22, 1979 if you will put your energy to the task between now and then.

## March 2, 2007
## Fort Lauderdale, Florida
## Doing the Impossible:
## Defeating the ERA

Thank you wonderful friends for being here tonight. I consider it a great honor to be part of Dr. Kennedy's Conference. I have admired him and been his friend since we were together on the public platform in the exciting year of 1980. And it is great that you are carrying on his work. Thank you for being here.

Tonight we're going to talk about a little bit of history. Doing the impossible: defeating the Equal Rights Amendment. It's been about 25 years since we celebrated the final burial of the Equal Rights Amendment, known as ERA.

The proposed amendment to the U.S. Constitution was advertised as a great benefit to women. Something that would rescue women from second-class citizenship. And for the first time, put *women* into the constitution. The ERA was passionately debated across America from 1972 to 1982. And then, the ERA was rejected by the American people. And the big lesson we learned from this is that in the marvelous process of self-government given to us by our founding fathers, it *is* possible for the people to defeat the entire political and media establishment. And to win despite incredible odds.

ERA passed Congress with only 23 out of 435 members of the House voting no. And passed the Senate with only eight out of 100 Senators voting no. And then it was sent out to the states on March 22, 1972. Within the first 12 months it was ratified in 30 states, and under our constitution they only needed eight more.

ERA has such a righteous name. Who could possibly oppose equal rights? And supporting ERA were all those who had pretensions to political power, from left to right, from Ted Kennedy to George Wallace, and three presidents of the United States Richard Nixon, Gerald Ford, and Jimmy Carter.

[Video clips] *President Nixon said today that he favors passage of the Equal Rights Amendment for Women. / The Equal Rights Amendment, which I wholeheartedly endorse, has not yet been ratified by the number of states necessary to make it a part of our Constitution. / We will not fail. We did not get in this fight to lose and we do not intend to lose. We will ratify the Equal Rights Amendment for the United States of America.*

ERA was actively supported by most of the pushy women's organizations, a consortium of 33 women's magazines, numerous Hollywood celebrities, and 99 percent of the media. But a little band of unflappable STOP ERA ladies in red had convened in my kitchen on the bluffs of the Mississippi River in Alton, Illinois, sent out to challenge all the big guns of modern politics.

We had no big names on our side. No presidents. No Governors. The Governors of North Carolina and Florida publicly demonstrated against us. There was only one lone senator of 100 who was willing to speak out against ERA, Watergate Senator Sam Ervin. And only three House members out of 435 dared to say a good word for our cause: Henry

Hyde, George Hansen, and Bob Dornan. None of the conservative magazines, journalists, and columnists we read today wrote helpful articles. We didn't have any friendly TV, radio, or talk show host. Everyone was hostile. There was no Rush Limbaugh talking about the femi-nazis. There was no FOX News to give balanced news and let the audience decide. There wasn't any no-spin zone. From the get go, we had to fight the semantics and the momentum.

Now ERA does not mention women. ERA calls for equality of rights on account of *sex*. Yet all of the reporters consistently called the ERA the equal rights for *women* amendment. Something to give *women* equal rights.

> [Video clips] *The House today by the overwhelming vote of 354 to 23 passed a proposed constitutional amendment to guarantee equal rights for women. / In other news, in a historic decision, the Senate voted 84-8 today to approve a constitutional amendment guaranteeing equal rights to women. The proposal goes to the states for ratification.*

Well, as Walter Cronkite would've said, that's the way it was.

Well, to get around big media, we didn't have any Internet, we didn't have fax machines. We only had the telephone and the *Phyllis Schlafly Report*. And our campaign was started with the February 1972 *Phyllis Schlafly Report*, called "What's Wrong with Equal Rights for Women?" Over the 10 years I wrote about 100 issues of my newsletter about ERA. And those reports staked out the battleground on which we engaged our adversaries. Mainly, the legal rights that women would lose if ERA were to ever ratify. And that strategic decision forced the feminists to spend their time attacking *me* and trying to answer the arguments in my newsletters.

We showed that ERA was a fraud. While pretending to benefit women, it actually would be a big takeaway of rights that women then possessed, such as the right of an 18-year-old girl not to be drafted and sent into military combat. And the right of a wife to be supported by her husband. We got our facts straight from the writings of the pro-ERA legal authorities: Yale Prof. Thomas I. Emerson's article in the Yale

Law journal, and ACLU lawyer Ruth Bader Ginsburg's federally financed book called *Sex Bias in the US Code*. These documents confirmed our arguments that ERA would draft women into combat, and abolish the presumption that the husband should take care of his wife and also take away the Social Security benefits of wives and widows. The ERA-ers could not show any benefit to women, not even in employment, since employment laws were already sex neutral.

The ERA-ers said their amendment would put women into the Constitution, but we showed that the Constitution doesn't mention men or women. It uses only sex-neutral words, such as we the people, person, citizen, Senator and President.

Now another document we used was "Revolution: Tomorrow is NOW." This was a publication of the National Organization for Women that set forth NOW's radical pro-abortion and anti-Christian agenda. We reprinted NOW's booklet and we sold it to raise funds for STOP ERA. We told people to be sure and read both sides of the story.

Well, we showed that ERA would give enormous power to the federal courts to define the words sex and equality

244

of rights. And Section 2 of ERA would give vast new powers to the Federal Government for all of the laws that make any differences of treatment between men and women on account of sex: marriage, property, divorce, alimony, adoptions, abortion, homosexual laws, sex crimes, private and public schools, boy and girl scouts, prison regulations, and insurance.

Now in September 1972, I invited 100 subscribers to the *Phyllis Schlafly Report* to meet me in St. Louis. We adopted the name STOP ERA and we selected our insignia, the stop sign. And then we all rode a bus down to the St. Louis Riverfront, where we dined on the Goldenrod Showboat. And I climbed up on the stage where so many melodramas have been performed, like my favorite one, *Showboat*. And I gave a speech on leadership and I invited these women not only to go home and defeat ERA, but also to become leaders in the conservative cause. And they did. All of the women were volunteers; we had no staff at that time. We recognized the worthy achievers with an Eagle Award and we presented them these awards for thanks for their volunteer work.

The women's liberation movement, which was then led by Gloria Steinem and Betty Friedan, was at the peak of its influence and enjoyed unparalleled access to the media. Betty Friedan started the women's liberation movement with her book, *The Feminine Mystique*, which whined about the alleged sad state of feminine wives. She founded the National Organization for Women, called NOW, to encourage women to be liberated from the home, husband, and children. The feminists favorite word became liberation.

My book called *Feminist Fantasies* is a wonderful refutation of feminist nonsense, about how American women are oppressed, a minority. My book ought to be used in these women studies courses as an antidote to all those tiresome tirades by the feminists.

While the media were solidly hostile to our cause, we knew the ERA-ers didn't have any solid arguments. We engaged them in debate whenever possible. Now in the 1970s, Phil Donahue had the biggest audience of anyone on television. He was even bigger than Oprah. So I went on the Donahue show to expose the liberation nonsense.

[Video clip] *Phil: Your daughter, then, is not going to be, sort of, trapped in a house.*

246

*Phyllis: Well, the house isn't trapping. Are you trying to tell me that it's "liberation" for a woman to go out and sit at a typewriter all day, or stand at a factory machine all day, instead of being in her own home where she can plan her own hours? You know, Phil, the Army has some new ads, some new billboards, out around, and the big headline says the Army has openings for cooks, and then they show a man and a woman standing in front of a big stack of potatoes in an Army kitchen. Now you're going to tell me it's "liberation" for a woman to leave her nice kitchen, with her stove and her sink and her refrigerator that her ever-loving husband bought for her, and go out and cook in an army kitchen and peel potatoes under the direction of some sergeant (and perish the thought if the sergeant is a woman!), and you tell me that's liberation? Why, that isn't liberation; liberation is in the home.*

Well, the feminists began to put me up against all of their heavyweights. In 1973, I did my first debate with Betty Friedan at Illinois State University. That's the one where Friedan famously said she'd like to burn me at the stake. She said other things that are too indecent to tell in mixed company. Over the years, I debated almost every prominent feminist and lectured on over 500 college campuses. It has been an experience.

Tom Snyder of *The Tomorrow Show* made a big effort to stage a TV debate with two couples facing off against each other. He had a terribly hard time finding any ERA advocate who had a husband, but he finally found one that we had never heard of, Brenda Feigen Fasteau. And we had a debate on television.

[Video clip] *Phyllis: The Equal Rights Amendment would impose a doctrinaire equality on men and women, and that's why we think it is a fraud because it will actually take away from women some of the important rights they now have by law. For example, it will take away women's right to be exempt from the draft and to be exempt from combat duty; it will take away the right of a wife to be supported by her husband in a home provided by her husband and her right to have her husband support her minor children.*

Take a good look at her. After the debate she left her husband and went to live with her lesbian girlfriend.

At state legislative hearings all during 1972, 1973, 1974, and 1975 we presented legislators with powerful arguments and documentation provided by the *Schlafly Report*. I ultimately trekked around to testify at 41 state hearings: in Little Rock, Arkansas; Richmond, Virginia; Jefferson City, Missouri; Atlanta, Georgia; Raleigh, North Carolina; Phoenix, Arizona; Columbia, South Carolina; Springfield, Illinois; Nashville, Tennessee; Tallahassee, Florida; Augusta, Maine; Montpelier, Vermont; Providence, Rhode Island; Denver, Colorado; Frankfort, Kentucky; Austin, Texas; Pierce, South Dakota; Bismarck, North Dakota; Carson City, Nevada; Dover, Delaware; Boise, Idaho; Indianapolis, Indiana; Topeka, Kansas; Lincoln, Nebraska; Columbus, Ohio; and Salt Lake City, Utah. I had to learn my state capitals. Those were experiences.

The draft was one of our best arguments in the early years because we were just coming out of the Vietnam War. The ERA-ers, most of whom were well over draft age, claimed that girls wanted to be drafted. Their leader Betty Friedan was emphatic about this.

> [Video clip] *Friedan: I have always felt and it seems to me the Americans must feel the equality of rights must mean the quality of responsibility and if there's ever a need for a draft again and there's no reason for women to be exempt on the basis of sex.*

They even got female members of Congress, such as Congresswoman Pat Schroeder, to assure us that ERA would definitely draft women into military combat.

> [Video clip] *Phyllis: The point is that under the Equal Rights Amendment, Congress will no longer have the option; Congress will be constitutionally required to draft women on the same basis as men.*
> *Host: Do you agree with that, Congresswoman Schroeder?*
> *Pat: I agree that we have the power, and whether or not we will continue to use it depends on the state of emergency.*

*Host: Do you agree that you will have no option if the Equal Rights Amendment passes?*

*Pat: That's right, we'll have to put laws in that apply both to males and females equally, and that—*

*Phyllis: Do you want to draft women?*

*Pat: —and that you can only draft women for combat duty if they can perform the same functions, and men and women would have to be equal.*

*Host: Do you think that's desirable?*

*Pat: Yes, I think that's all right.*

We made so many trips to the state capitals, and I gave directions with my bullhorn. One day a preacher rented a monkey suit and joined our demonstration walking around with the sign that said, "don't monkey with the Constitution." He almost lost his church over that.

The feminists were usually belligerent towards the legislators, whereas we were always ladies. We sent them Valentines and Easter cards, and messages like this, "for recognizing the difference you are terrific, fabulous, sensational, fantastic, and marvelous." Every year, our ladies baked a loaf of homemade bread and took it to every one of our

236 state legislators. The feminists called that our dirty trick. Of course most feminists were not capable of baking a loaf of bread.

In 1976, I led a group of STOP ERA women to do something that none of us had ever done before. We picketed the White House to protest Betty Ford lobbying for the ERA.

> [Video clip] *First Lady Betty Ford has been actively campaigning for the constitutional amendment to provide equal rights for women, even to the point of telephoning state legislators. About thirty-five pickets showed up at the White House today to protest her activity, but Mrs. Ford told reporters she's sticking to her guns.*

Well, the next year I led a picket line in front of the White House to protest Rosalynn Carter lobbying for ERA.

> [Video clip] *Rosalynn: Time is running out, and we, we just have to get the Equal Rights Amendment ratified; it's too important to just let it drift away.*

But media and political pressures in favor of ERA were so powerful that hardly anybody believed ERA could be defeated. Legislators were intimidated by the constant drumbeat, the razzmatazz of celebrities, such as Alan Alda and Betty Ford, and by big money, and by the loud mouth feminists such as Eleanor Smeal.

[Video clip] *Song: "ERA! ERA! – We Want it Now! We Want it Now!*

That was intimidating to legislators.

Illinois was a frontline of the battle. And the ERA-ers had all the big political guns on their side: the governor, Illinois Senate and House leadership, and the media. And we desperately needed an event. Something spectacular to convince the legislators that American women really opposed ERA. I prayed we could bring 1,000 people to our state capital to rally against ERA; something that had never been done before happened in Springfield, Illinois.

I sent out the message to all the Churches: the Protestants and Evangelicals, the Catholics, the Mormons, and the Orthodox Jews. And April 27, 1976, was the day that changed the face of politics forever. A thousand people did come to Springfield, from all over Illinois. Many riding on buses that read "Joy" and "Jesus Saves." I gave directions on my bullhorn in the rotunda. Many of our people carried babies in their arms or homemade signs, and we hand-delivered our homemade bread to every legislator.

That thrilling STOP ERA rally in Springfield in 1976 turned the tide against ERA in Illinois. On that momentous day, we invented the pro-family movement by persuading believers of all denominations to do things that most of them had never done before. They came into the political process for the first time and they began to work together with other religious faiths for a political goal they shared, mainly protection of the family in the United States Constitution against the radical feminists. We did not have one single big political name at our rally, but that rally, nevertheless, morphed our STOP ERA committee into the nucleus of the mighty pro-family movement that is so powerful today.

Now, the pro-ERA-ers responded with their own rally. And these are pictures taken of that pro-ERA rally; pictures that showed their ranks were filled with lesbians, abortion activists, socialist workers and party members, radicals of all kinds, and other unkempt persons.

Nevertheless, most of the prominent Illinois politicians attended *their* rally, not ours. The ERA-ers displayed their radical streaks in other states too. In Virginia, the ERA-ers spit on the Speaker of the House, staged a sit-down at the state capital in Richmond, and had to be carried out by the police.

[Video clip] *ERA supporters were arrested after they protested defeat in the committee of the Virginia Legislature.*

Among other nasty tactics, the ERA-ers hired a professional pie thrower, who hit me in the face with an apple pie when I was at the Waldorf Astoria in New York City receiving an award from the National Republican Club.

Now in the fall of 1977, our cause appeared hopeless, especially because the feminists were able to use government offices and taxpayers money to promote ERA. The ERA campaign was run right out of the war room of President

Carter's White House, and lady state legislators were invited to the White House to be lobbied personally by the Carters. Bella Abzug was a member of Congress, and she got Congress to appropriate $5 million for a tax-funded feminist convention in Houston in November 1977, called International Women's Year. It was designed to be a massive media event that would help to ratify ERA in the remaining states. The International Women's Year Convention opened in Houston. They had three first ladies on the platform: Rosalynn Carter, Betty Ford, and Ladybird Johnson. That's the kind of power they were able to put out for their event. And every feminist you've ever heard of was there at that November 1977 convention in Houston. They tell me there were 3,000 members of the media on hand to give them massive press and television coverage.

But after they cheered and resolved for ERA, they locked ERA into their other demands: taxpayer funding of abortions and the entire gay-rights agenda. You see the ERA-ers believed that since abortion is something that happens only to women, it is sex discrimination to deny taxpayer funding for abortions. And since the word used in ERA is not women but is sex, ERA would require us to grant same-sex marriage licenses. So, the famous Bella Abzug presided at that raucous convention, and you'll see Betty Friedan shouting from the floor.

> [Sound clip] *Madam Chairperson, I move the adoption of the following resolutions: the Equal Rights Amendment should be ratified. / I would like to ask this body to give the most resounding and urgent vote demanding the ratification of the Equal Rights Amendment within the coming year! Because, otherwise, the enormous expenditure of energy and money and effort that has brought us to this point will be in vain, and these ten years of movement will be in vain. / The question arises on the adoption of the resolution: all those in favor would you please rise. / Snake dance through the hall [background chanting] ERA! ERA! / We support the U.S. Supreme Court decisions, which guarantee reproductive freedom to women. / The resolution on reproductive freedom is adopted. / Madam Chair, I move the following resolution on sexual preference. Congress, state, and local legislatures should enact legislation to eliminate discrimination on the basis of sexual and affectional preference in areas including, but not limited to,*

*employment, housing, public accommodations, credit,*
*public facilities, government funding in the military.*

They published a book setting forth their demands. But after the feminists released their balloons and pranced around with their lesbian placards, the whole country realized why they were pushing so hard for the ERA, and who was doing the pushing. Here are some pictures from the booths and signs at that feminist convention. And the most popular buttons worn at the feminist conference were the ones that said, "a woman without a man is like a fish without a bicycle," and "mother nature is a lesbian." At booths you could also pick up booklets on what lesbians do.

A couple of months later, a reporter asked the governor of Missouri, "Governor, are you for ERA?" And he replied, "do you mean the old ERA or the new ERA? I was for equal pay for equal work, but after those women went down to Houston and got tangled up with the abortionists and the lesbians, I can tell you ERA will never pass in the Show Me state."

Houston gave us the proof that ERA's real agenda is taxpayer-funded abortions and gay rights. And since that feminist convention, ERA has been voted on about 25 times in state legislatures, Congress, and several statewide referendums, and it has never had another victory.

Nevertheless, the fight went on. To counteract that tax-funded atrocity our Eagle Forum Board took another call in Houston at the same time in the Astro Arena. We urged our people to come from all over the country (at their own expense, of course). We called it the pro-family rally and looking back I don't know how we had the nerve to make a contract for a hall that seated 15,000 people. We just knew we had to make a statement.

From all over the country, our women rode on buses up to 20 hours each way. They came to our pro-family rally and then returned home on the buses without ever going to bed. The buses came and they came and they came. And we filled the Astro Arena to overflowing. November 19, 1977, was the day the expression pro-family movement went into the political vocabulary. The *Houston Post* reported, "an attendance of 20,000 people in the hall that could only seat 15,000." Bob

Dornan was the only national celebrity who dared to come to our rally.

> [Sound clip] *Phyllis: In order to have held the line for the last five years against the tremendous odds of White House lobbying, federal government expenditures, prominent people, and big money, we had to have somebody on our side who was more powerful than the President of the United States.*

When ERA was voted out of Congress in 1972, it was given a specific deadline of seven years. When the ERA-ers realized they were running out of time, President Carter and Congress gave them a crooked three-year time extension. The political cartoonists had a field day describing the extension as giving three more innings to a baseball game that was not tied up. Now we considered the original seven-year deadline the constitutional termination of the ERA. So, in 1979, we loudly proclaimed that we had won. That the ERA was dead.

> [Video clip] *Host: What's the problem with the ERA, Mrs. Schlafly? In your view, what bothers you the most about the possibility of its passing?*

*Phyllis: The Equal Rights Amendment is a big takeaway of women's rights. When the seven-year deadline given to the ERA passed without ratification, this was the greatest victory for women's rights since the women's suffrage amendment of the 1920s because this means that women will be able to defend you and your daughters from being drafted and sent into combat.*

We had to make a magnificent burial party at the Shoreham Hotel in Washington, D.C. on March 22, 1979. To celebrate, we named the title of our gala "The End of the ERA," and that was a double play on words because it was also the end of an era; the era of conservative defeats. We proclaimed that we had actually won; that we had beaten ERA. We gave life to the conservative movement and taught conservatives the lesson that it is really possible to win political battles. And the key to winning was to combine the fiscal conservatives with the new social conservatives; the people who cared about pro-life and about ERA who we brought out of the churches. And then a year later, in 1980, this new conservative pro-family coalition won a tremendous victory by electing Ronald Reagan our President.

But the fight went on in the three extended years. And the ERA-ers staged huge media events with celebrities, such as Phil Donahue, Marlo Thomas, and Alan Alda, who came personally to Springfield, Illinois.

> [Video clip] *For the past 5 years, the fight over the Equal Rights Amendment has been increasing in pitch and has become one of the volatile issues in the US today. / How long can we stand by and watch qualified people denied their fair share in the economy and the political strength of the nation, JUST because they're women?*

Well, during the extension period, the ERA-ers staged huge media events with these kinds of celebrities—you saw that impressive demonstration. All our Illinois votes were cliffhangers. We won with the changing mix of conservative and liberal republicans and democrats, downstate rural guys and Chicago-machine Democrats. The most dramatic Illinois vote came on June 18, 1980. Tension was very high and all the national media showed up with their cameras. President Jimmy Carter was telephoning Democratic legislators and promising them federal housing projects in their district if they would vote yes on ERA. Republican Governor James Thompson was telephoning Republican legislators and promising dams, roads, and bridges in their districts if they would vote yes. Mayor Jane Byrne was telephoning Chicago legislators and forcing them to vote yes under threat of firing them and their relatives from city patronage jobs. Democratic legislators who are beholden to the Chicago machine wept publicly as they apologized to me for having to vote yes so their relatives wouldn't lose their jobs. And then there were even cash bribes flowing. One feminist was finally later convicted of offering a cash bribe to one of the legislators for a yes vote.

It was exciting on that day when the vote climbed electronically on the panel in the House Chamber. A great shout went up when it became clear that we defeated ERA again. I was standing in the gallery of the Illinois House when ABC Nightline put NOW President, Eleanor Smeal, in front of the cameras and said, "Ms. Smeal, you said you had the votes. What happened?" And she replied, "there's something very powerful against us and I certainly don't mean people." Smeal didn't know what that power was, but we knew. It was prayer and the truth. We had done all we could … but the punch line is we had done all we could and the Lord brought us two votes from Chicago legislators who had never voted our way before.

One of the biggest battles in our ERA fight was the Republican National Convention in Detroit in 1980. ERA had been in the Republican platform for many years and I was determined to take it out so that Ronald Reagan would not be embarrassed by the feminists. But that wasn't easy. The ERA-ers were organized and noisy. They had all the media and most important Republican officials on their side. Their spokesman was Congresswoman Margaret Heckler.

[Video clips] *Supporters of the Equal Rights Amendment, about 5,000 of them, marched outside of the convention hall threatening to paint lines of discord across the picture of harmony the Reagan forces want to portray here. ERA supporters have not given up. In fact, they are working on a new strategy to add ERA to the party's platform. A strategy that calls for lining up six votes for majority support for ERA. / Just judging from the enormous outpouring of amazement and shock and dismay, across America, over the Republican party's refusal to reaffirm the ERA, I would say that millions of votes are at stake on this issue.*

Well, indeed, millions of votes were at stake. And they voted for Ronald Reagan. And Ronald Reagan assured me that he was against ERA.

Well, on January 3, 1982, Oklahoma defeated ERA for the last time. On June 4, North Carolina defeated the ERA for the last time. And the disgruntled pro-ERA-ers sent disgusting bags of chicken manure to the 23 senators who voted no.

Time was running out for ERA, but the ERA-ers never ran out of money. In the last weeks they spend $15 million on the TV advertising campaign featuring Hollywood celebrities, such as Ed Asner and Archie Bunker. Now since they didn't have a single good argument for ERA, you can see how stupid their ad was.

[Video clips] *Various celebrities: "Help pass ERA."*

Well you can see they had no arguments, and of course that was one of the things about ERA. They could never show

265

any benefit to women whatsoever. Fortunately that $15 million ad did not persuade any legislators to vote yes.

On June 21, Florida defeated ERA for the last time. I'm sure there's some here who helped in a battle. Illinois was forced to vote on ERA every year for 10 years, and the last year things got very ugly as the battle continued. In April, the excommunicated Mormon Sonia Johnson started a hunger strike in the state capital, and she was joined by Dick Gregory and other experienced hunger strikers, making it a big media event. And then a chain-gang of pro-ERA-ers chained themselves to the door of the senate chambers.

> [Video clips] *ERA lobbyists tried to embarrass the Illinois legislature into a favorable vote. Seven women are into their third week of a hunger strike and 15 others have chained themselves to the entrance of the state senate since last Thursday. / Betty Ford: In the history of the Equal Rights Amendment, we've never been so close. I can't wait and I want to be there when the dream of equality becomes a reality.*

Well, ERA supporters then went to the slaughterhouse and bought plastic bags of pig's blood and came back and wrote on our marble floors of the state capital the names of the legislators they hated the most. Fortunately, those tactics did not persuade our legislators to vote yes, and Illinois finally dealt the deathblow to ERA.

> [Video clips] *Within a year, 30 states had ratified the amendment. It seemed that nothing could stop it, but Phyllis Schlafly changed the course of ERA.*
> *Phyllis: And it would be a direct attack on our families, on our morals, on our culture.*
> *Host: She created and led the STOP ERA movement.*
> *Phyllis: As soon as the state legislature started to have hearings and we began to have equal time, it was obvious that the people didn't want it and that it could be defeated.*
> *Host: From her home, she mobilized fifty thousand housewives into a conservative strike force. Her women delivered flowers to legislators and closely monitored voting records on ERA.*

So, June 30, 1982, 1,500 battle-weary, but triumphant STOP ERA volunteers gathered again in the ballroom of the Shoreham Hotel in Washington to celebrate our second and final burial of ERA at midnight. A giant rainbow of balloons rose high over the dais, and then many political personages including President Reagan paid tribute.

The heroes of the day were the women who came from the 15 states that never ratified ERA, plus the five states that bravely rescinded their previous ratifications.

> [Video clips] *Phyllis: We have them out there, they have stood the test and we can build this into a mighty movement that can set America on the right path. We need your help in this effort and conquer we must for the cause it is just. And this be our motto, in God is our trust. And we have the strength of character and this battle we have waged has proved it. Thank you for being here.*

The evening closed with singing "The Impossible Dream." We had truly one and impossible battle and defeated the unbeatable foe.

Thank you for coming.

# 1994
## Virginia
## The Future of the Republican Party, Like Its Past, is Pro-Life

T hank you, Bill, for arranging this platform to discuss the future of the Republican Party and pro-life. I have a great interest in the future of the Republican party. I've been a Republican volunteer all my life and was an elected delegate to six Republican National Conventions and elected alternate delegate to two others.

The Republican Party is not a fraternity with a hazing procedure for admission. We impose no ideological or religious tests on anyone who calls himself a Republican and we invite all Americans to vote for our candidates. We do not demand to know the reasons why people vote for Republican candidates and there is no space in those little boxes on the ballot to record their reasons.

Nevertheless the Republican Party has a tradition of standing for certain principles. And it has and should have an identity different from the other parties. The Republican Party was born on the principle that no human being should be considered the property of another. That is our heritage as Republicans and it would be a tragic mistake to abandon that fundamental precept now.

The most famous political debates in American history, the Lincoln-Douglas debates of 1858, will be reenacted this year on C-SPAN. During those seven debates up and down the state of Illinois, Abraham Lincoln enunciated and pressed the position of the then-new Republican Party that slavery was a moral and a social and a political wrong.

Stephen A. Douglas took the position that individual states should have freedom of choice to decide this issue for themselves through the democratic process, without dictate from the federal government. In Quincy, Illinois, he even argued that "we should deal with slavery as with any other wrong insofar as we can prevent its growing larger and deal with it in that. In the run of time there may be some promise of an end of it. We have a due regard for the actual presence of it amongst us and the difficulties of getting rid of it in any satisfactory way. But we must oppose it as an evil." Where did Lincoln get his authority for saying that slavery was wrong and must be eliminated eventually if not immediately? It was from our nation's founding documents, the Declaration of Independence which has served as a self-evident truth that each of us is endowed by their Creator with inalienable rights of life and liberty. And that government is instituted for the purpose of securing those rights.

Douglas countered with the arguments of choice, states rights and opposition to dictation by the federal government. He argued that "Each state of this union has a right to do as it pleases on the subject of slavery." Douglas supported the Dred Scott decision saying, "I choose to abide by the decisions of the Supreme Court as they are pronounced." Lincoln said that he "looks forward to a time when slavery shall be abolished everywhere." Douglas replied, "I look forward to a time when each state shall be allowed to do as it pleases. If it chooses to keep slavery forever it is not my business. But if it chooses to abolish slavery that it is its own business not mine. I care more for the great principle of self-government." In reporting the

Lincoln-Douglas debates, the biased press of the 1830s called Lincoln, "A dead dog walking to his political grave" and reported Douglas' arguments as "logical and powerful." Lincoln lost that senatorial election to Douglas. But two years later, Abraham Lincoln was elected our first Republican president and the verdict of history is that Lincoln's argument was correct. The real issue in this controversy, Lincoln said in the Alton, Illinois debate, is that the Republican Party "looks upon the institution of slavery as a wrong. And the Democratic Party does not look upon it as a wrong."

Lincoln proclaimed the slavery issue represented, "The eternal struggle between these two principles. Right and wrong."

Abortion is the right or wrong issue of our times. We should parallel the words of Abraham Lincoln today and say the Republican Party looks upon abortion as a wrong. And the Democratic Party does not look upon it as a wrong. That's the crucial difference between the two parties in the 1990s. The Republican Party must not adopt the Stephen Douglas position that democracy or states' rights can have the power to deprive individual human beings of their Creator-endowed right to life.

We must not adopt the Stephen Douglas position that a bad Supreme Court decision is irrevocable or infallible. The Declaration of Independence does not mention slavery. But in the Galesburg, Illinois debate, Lincoln pointed to the clear meaning of the Declaration's words that all of us are endowed with inalienable rights. And he challenged Douglas that "the entire record of the world from the date of the Declaration of Independence up to three years ago may be searched in vain for one single affirmation from one single man that the Negro was not included in the Declaration of Independence."

Likewise the Declaration of Independence does not mention abortion. But you will search in vain for a single affirmation that the Creator-endowed right to life was to be withheld from a baby until the moment of birth. Every new advance in science, especially the DNA and the ultrasound photographs of babies in the womb, confirms that the unique individual identity of each of us is present, a human, alive and growing, before the mother knows she is pregnant. Roe v. Wade, combined with its companion case Dover v. Bolton, legalized the terminations of the unborn baby throughout nine months of pregnancy. And that effectively makes the baby the property of the mother. That proposition is inconsistent with respect for individual human life. Some suggest that we should compromise our traditional Republican principles and diffuse the issue by taking popular positions on subsidiary issues. But a party platform is not a piece of legislation and should not attempt to be. A platform is a standard, a banner to raise on high, to proclaim our general principles and display our convictions. The Republican Party must show virility in its principles. That's what sets us apart from the Democrats. We should be strong on strategic principle, while leaving the details and the tactics to the legislative process. The Republican Party, speaking through its platforms adopted at its quadrennial conventions, has in varying language consistently upheld the right to life of unborn babies ever since the 1973 Roe v. Wade decision.

Unfortunately, the liberal media have used the technique known as false memory syndrome to try to rewrite the history of the 1992 Republican National Convention and November election. The liberal media have even misrepresented the text of the pro-life plank in our platform. It was identical to the plank Bush won on in 1988 and substantially the same as Reagan won on in 1984. The Republican Party's pro-life positions were arrived at through the democratic process and maintained their consistency through five Republican National Conventions. There is no realistic prospect of that changing. Those who want to remove the pro-life position had every opportunity to participate in the 1992 primary and Convention caucus process and elect their delegates. But even with ample money and media reinforcement they failed to make any significant impact on the pro-life convention. A majority at the 1992 National Convention were those who wanted to remove the pro-life plank and they needed only six out of fifty state delegations to precipitate a floor fight on the abortion issue. They were only able to get two of our fifty states.

Yet the media clamor persists that the Republican Party should acquiesce in the ban or at least modifying its pro-life position. To do that would not only be wrong, it would not only be a betrayal of our honorable tradition, but it would be politically stupid. And since in politics perception is reality waffling would be perceived as abandonment. It is a fatal mistake for a politician or a party to reverse its position for pragmatic reasons.

In 1992, George Bush gave us a bitter lesson in the high cost of reneging on a major campaign promise. The Republican Party cannot afford to repeat the Bush mistake. Even President Clinton has taken a beating from the pro-Clinton media for his foreign policy reversals, even when he should have reversed himself.

All of the election data confirms that the pro-life position was a big plus, not a minus for the Republican Party in the 1992 election. The four major television networks hired voter research and surveys to do massive exit polls on Election Day, November 3, 1992. These polls confirm the obvious—that the economy, especially the tax increases following the broken "read my lips" promise, was the reason George Bush lost the election. More importantly, the exit polls also show that of the 12 percent for whom the issue of abortion decided their vote, 56 percent voted for Bush and only 36 percent for Clinton. That made pro-life a measurable three to five point advantage for Republicans. The pro-life advantage was actually even greater than those figures because another 15 percent of voters told the exit pollsters that family values determined their vote and those people voted for Bush over Clinton by three to one, 66 percent to 23 percent.

Some people get down on their knees every night and ask the good Lord to remove abortion from the political sphere. But all the incantations cannot take abortion out of public controversy. It is a national, moral issue because it confronts the fundamental issues of right and wrong. Of life and death. It is a social issue because it goes to the most deeply held part of human relationships and our respect for the worth of our fellow human beings. And it is a political issue because every year dozens of bills about abortion are introduced into the Congress and the state legislatures. And every public official must vote on those bills.

Remembering that the 1996 Republican platform will be written by delegates who will not be elected for two more years and the 1992 platform is not open to amendments, I offer the following language to be considered as a platform statement again.

The Republican Party was founded on the principle that no human being should be considered the property of another, and on a repudiation of the Dred Scott decision by the U.S. Supreme Court which had ruled otherwise. Our first

Republican President Abraham Lincoln relied on our nation's founding document, the Declaration of Independence, for authority to uphold the Creator-endowed inalienable right of life and liberty of every individual, and the proposition that government has the duty to protect that right.

The Republican Party continues to uphold the principle that every human being born and unborn, young and old, healthy and disabled, has a fundamental individual right to life. We rely on the Declaration of Independence for authority in asserting that every individual human being has a Creator-endowed right to life, and that it is the duty of government to protect that life. In the tradition of Abraham Lincoln we assert that no human being born or unborn can be considered the property of another. And we repudiate the Roe v. Wade decision by the U.S. Supreme Court which held otherwise by presuming to give some individuals the so-called right to terminate the life of others. We reaffirm our support for the appointment of judges who respect the sanctity of human life. We will work to restore the right to life to the class of human beings from whom it has been unjustly taken away. And we oppose all efforts to legitimatize or finance with public revenues the deprivation of that right.

Thank you. Thank you. Thank you.

# September 10, 2016
# St. Louis
# Her Lamp Would Not Go Out

*Remarks delivered by John Schlafly at the funeral of his mother, Phyllis Schlafly, at the Cathedral Basilica of St. Louis on September 10, 2016.*

When my father, Fred Schlafly, reached the age of 75, and realized he could no longer compete in the sports he had enjoyed throughout his life, he turned to my mother one day and said, "Phyllis, you probably have about 10 good years left."

That conversation took place more than 30 years ago. And those 30 extra years were good years: good for us, of course, her family and friends who received her wise counsel; and also good for our country, as her political activism continued to influence the 2016 election.

They were good years for Phyllis, too, despite the increasing burdens of her old age. She was able to watch her family grow to 25 descendants, with more on the way. In her final days, she had the great joy of seeing the infants and toddlers that my father never knew.

My parents were partners in their life together, and Phyllis depended on Fred for everyday reinforcement. He supported her career, screened what she wrote, and coached her on what to say. She called him "the censor."

Fred Schlafly's influence is apparent in Phyllis' most widely read article, "What's Wrong With 'Equal Rights' for Women?" First published in February 1972, that article has since been reprinted in dozens of college textbooks and is considered the classic expression of Phyllis' opposition to feminism.

The 1972 article set forth the proposition that our public laws and policies, as embedded in the fundamental law of our nation, should reinforce the family as the basic unit of any society. Confronting the burgeoning feminist movement and its principal objective, the Equal Rights Amendment (ERA),

Phyllis' simple but powerful argument seemed controversial and even retrograde to liberals.

As Father Brian Harrison explained in his homily today, the idea that a nation's laws should recognize the basic social unit as the family, rather than the individual, is grounded in the social teaching of the Catholic church. It's the central insight of the pope's famous 1891 encyclical Rerum Novarum, which launched Catholic social teaching, and it has been reaffirmed many times since then.

Phyllis expressed the idea in a way that attracted tens of thousands of people, mostly of other faiths, to what she called the "pro-family" movement. Many of those she touched and inspired have honored our family by coming here today. We now take Phyllis to rest beside her husband, my father, in the place she selected many years ago. Like every place she ever lived, she decided the burial plot needed another tree — a maple tree that turns bright gold in the fall.

She selected a tree, planted it and drove there frequently with buckets of water, to make sure the tree survived. Since we buried my father there, 23 years ago, the little tree that Phyllis planted has become a powerful, majestic, stately canopy, and next month its color will be gorgeous.

Reflecting on my mother's long life, the singular quality that explains her effectiveness is that she was <u>always</u> prepared. Whether her task was to give a speech, conduct a meeting, or meet a deadline, her careful preparation made the job seem effortless and gave her time to deal with unexpected events.

Phyllis was never at a loss for the appropriate words. She faced crisis and conflict with grace, and she infuriated opponents with her unflappable good humor.

In the parable of the bridegroom (Matt. 25:1-13), Jesus tells the story of 10 women who were called to light the way for a wedding party. Five of the women brought no extra oil, and their lamps went out before the wedding party arrived.

The other five women came prepared with extra oil in case the wedding party was running late. The sensible five were admitted to the wedding feast from which the foolish five were excluded.

Phyllis would have been one of the five wise enough to bring an extra flask of oil. Even in her final year, she was planning for the future, including America's future as well as her own.

Phyllis Schlafly was a wise woman, a sensible woman, a faithful woman. Her lamp would not go out, and I believe she was prepared for today.

$$\displaystyle \infty$$

## September 21, 2016
## Reflections on My Mother
### *By Andy Schlafly*

Phyllis Schlafly was with us a glorious 92 years, and active in politics for more than 70 of them. It is difficult to identify any issue that she was not on the right side of, typically years or decades before others rallied beside her.

She wrote or spoke out on nearly every controversial American political matter, and the conservative movement today is based largely on work that she did five, ten, twenty, and even sixty years ago. Though we grieve her passing, she leaves us with a legacy that will take us our own lifetimes to fully appreciate.

Donald Trump, in his remarkable eulogy to Phyllis last Saturday at the beginning of her funeral, observed that Phyllis has shaped American politics for more than one-quarter of its entire existence. He commented that she always put America first, as he does, and the massive crowd of attendees gave a standing ovation to Trump in immense gratitude to him for so honoring Phyllis.

Phyllis wrote a bestselling book in 1964 called *A Choice Not An Echo*, which foreshadowed Trump's meteoric rise. The book exposed how the political system is rigged by kingmakers, and she was thrilled by the arrival of Trump as a candidate for president, 52 years after publication of her work, to take on and defeat the kingmakers in the Republican Party.

Phyllis anticipated and led on so many political issues that it would require another book just to list them. Her *Phyllis Schlafly Report*, now in its 50th year, is probably the longest continuing political newsletter in history, and its inaugural edition discussed the importance of our Panama Canal a full decade before that became a hot issue propelling Ronald Reagan to his successful campaign for president.

In defeating the Equal Rights Amendment, the work for which Phyllis is most famous, she took an initially unpopular stance years before others joined her. Her successful STOP

ERA effort did more to define the conservative movement today than any other struggle.

But unlike most political leaders, Phyllis also had a tremendous cultural influence, by establishing respectability for those who stay at home and raise their children. Even many liberal-leaning women who attained adulthood in the 1980s and beyond are grateful to Phyllis for carving out space in our culture for them to spend some time away from the rat race to raise their children, and educate them at home.

Indeed, one of Phyllis's proudest achievements was that she taught her children how to read at home, which she did for all six of them in the 1950s and 1960s. This was decades before the homeschooling movement blossomed as an expansion on the same concept.

Recently some have called Phyllis the "Iron Lady," but that term fails to capture the enormous good humor and charm that she always had in the face of intense hostility. Many middle-aged people today had the benefit of attending a debate or presentation by Phyllis on a college campus, where she would invariably withstand a hostile opponent or audience with remarkable grace.

The funeral Mass on Saturday was held at the Cathedral Basilica in St. Louis, the same place where Phyllis was married in 1949 to Fred Schlafly, a blissful union that lasted until his death in 1993. But far from slowing down as a widow, Phyllis continued her work for another 23 years by both building on her prior efforts and expanding into new topics.

For example, she wrote her book on *The Supremacists* in 2004 to explain the growing problem of judicial supremacy, which foreshadowed the shocking court decisions in recent years and the crisis that we face in this election as the replacement for Justice Scalia hinges on the outcome. Her more recent book on *No Higher Power: Obama's War on Religious Freedom* (2012) exposed the anti-Christian agenda of the Obama Administration.

Phyllis attended Republican National Conventions over a span of 64 years, from 1952 to 2016, and I had the joy of being with her for nearly two weeks in Cleveland this summer at her final convention. The party platform now embraces

Phyllis's positions on everything from building a wall to stop illegal immigration, to being strongly pro-life, to attaining military superiority, which were all positions that she staked out decades ago.

Phyllis never stopped writing, speaking, and organizing. The very day after her passing away on September 5th, the anniversary of Mother Teresa's death, Phyllis's 27th book was released, *The Conservative Case for Trump*.

William Shakespeare left this world with a legacy in playwriting that took generations to admire fully. Phyllis Schlafly produced more during her lifetime than the rest of us could keep up with, and it may take us decades simply to realize all the good work that Phyllis, the "conservative hero" in the words of Trump's eulogy, has left us with.

*Andy Schlafly, an attorney, is the fifth of Phyllis Schlafly's six children.*

## About Phyllis Schlafly

Phyllis Schlafly was a national leader of the conservative movement since the publication of her best-selling 1964 book, *A Choice Not An Echo* which was updated and re-issued in 2014. She was a leader of the pro-family movement since 1972, when she started her national volunteer organization called Eagle Forum. The *Ladies' Home Journal* named her one of the 100 most important women of the 20th century.

Mrs. Schlafly is the author or editor of 27 books and served as a member of the Commission on the Bicentennial of the U.S. Constitution, 1985-1991, appointed by President Reagan. She has testified before more than 50 Congressional and State Legislative committees on constitutional, national defense, and family issues.

Phyllis Schlafly is America's best-known advocate of the dignity and honor that we as a society owe to the role of full-time homemaker. The mother of six children, she was the

1992 Illinois Mother of the Year. She passed away on September 5, 2016.

## About Ed Martin

On September 28, 2015, Phyllis Schlafly named Ed Martin as her hand-picked successor. Ed had been working as a special assistant to Phyllis for more than two years. A lawyer and bioethicist by training, Ed had previously served as chairman of the Missouri Republican Party and chief of staff to Missouri Governor Matt Blunt. Ed lives in St. Louis, Missouri, with his wife and four children.

*It is important to thank the following people who are so important in this work and in Phyllis' work over the past years: John Schlafly, JoAnn Jouett, and Georgia Wolters who work at Eagle Trust; Rebekah Gantner, Gwen Kelley, Deb Pentecost, Ryan Hite, and Caroline Corley who work at the Eagle Forum Education and Legal Defense Fund; and Kathleen Sullivan who served Phyllis so well over the past year.*

*Ed Martin*

*Dec. 2016*